CW01467678

*Front cover: Ex-Services Campaign for Nuclear Disarmament
demonstration, Edinburgh, organised by the author and led by
Air Commodore Alistair Mackie and Councillor Mary Mulligan.*

ONE STEP FORWARD, TWO STEPS BACK?

The Social History of a Left-Wing Activist – A Case Study

Ray Newton

MINERVA PRESS

LONDON
ATLANTA MONTREUX SYDNEY

ONE STEP FORWARD, TWO STEPS BACK?
The Social History of a Left-Wing Activist – A Case Study
Copyright © Ray Newton 1998

All Rights Reserved

No part of this book may be reproduced in any form,
by photocopying or by any electronic or mechanical means,
including information storage or retrieval systems,
without permission in writing from both the copyright owner
and the publisher of this book.

ISBN 0 75410 086 3

First Published 1998 by
MINERVA PRESS
195 Knightsbridge
London SW7 1RE

Printed in Great Britain for Minerva Press

ONE STEP FORWARD, TWO STEPS BACK?

The Social History of a Left-Wing Activist – A Case Study

Dedicated to my grandchildren and the generations who will have to solve the problems we have bequeathed to them.

Contents

Chapter I
The Personal is Political

> The sum of my politics is to try and support whatever social order is capable of reducing, even marginally, the aggregate of hatred and of pain in the human circumstance.
>
> George Steiner
> *Errata; an examined life*

All my life I seem to have been questioning the views of the establishment and demonstrating against them. Some questions have been answered but many have not; instead they have provoked other questions. Is socialism dead? Does man make history or does history make man? How much of us is the result of nature and how much of nurture? To what extent do our personal relationships and morality reflect those of society at large? What about the inexorable march of progress, however we define this? How effective can we be as individuals in helping people to help themselves? Does each generation have to learn afresh by experience the problems and contradictions inherent in the human condition? How, in fact, do we live in harmony with ourselves and others?

In asking these questions we make assumptions and these have changed during the century in which I have had the privilege of living. They involve false dichotomies (e.g. nature v. nurture), changing attitudes (e.g. to morality), and much more.

First, let's consider the idea of progress. The exponentially increasing wealth and productivity that we have seen during my lifetime has led people to believe in the inevitability of progress, of development, of a steady increase in their standard of living and of better health, recreational and transport facilities for all. The Marxist view went along with this perception but invoked the class struggle in order to achieve these advances. We also talked of uneven development in both time and space, and of replacing the jungle warfare of capitalism with the more humane, people-centred socialism, based on a philosophy of not merely interpreting the world but of changing it. We held the view that man had evolved, developed social organisation and progressed in terms of individual self-fulfilment, in a series of dialectical jumps – simplified by the catchphrase 'Two steps forward, one step back'. The ebb and flow of struggles within and between societies eventually resulted in a positive outcome. We rejected a 'spontaneous' view of progress but were sure of the advance of civilisation and the opportunity to better the whole of mankind. Now we are not so sure. Vast increases in industrial production have resulted in unacceptable levels of pollution, the depletion of non-renewable resources, soil erosion, global warming, refugees, violence and a downward spiral leading to ecological catastrophe in the twenty-first century.

In 1940 T.S. Eliot prophetically wrote, 'A good deal of our material progress is a progress for which succeeding generations may have to pay dearly.' Our personal progress and material advancement may be hiding the unpalatable fact that the planet will no longer be able to accommodate and adapt to the massive pressures on its ecosystem without dire consequences to its human population. If this is so, we may now be entering a new situation in which we should think in terms of 'One step forward, two steps back' and challenge the notion of inevitable progress. This is the theme running through my mind as I write these memoirs, but we should be optimistic in our ability, at least, to make this one step forward – to light a candle instead of cursing the darkness.

We also assumed that 'leaders' equipped with the new ideology would know how to use their newly found power wisely. Surely they would work in the interests of the vast majority and not of themselves? Surely priority would be given to a more equitable distribution of vastly increased resources? Our aim then, as today, was to rectify the obscenity of widespread poverty and misery of a world in which twenty-six per cent of its population takes ninety-six per cent of its health resources.

Such glaring inequalities are increasing, and those in a position to redistribute wealth on a fairer basis, whether in government or on the boards of transnational corporations, are intent on doing just the opposite. They claim that only market forces can enable society to function and that people must be motivated by money and power. The role of interest groups, vested in perpetuating their power and privilege, was illustrated by the showing of an advert on one American TV station in 1996 by a conservation organisation. The advert was then refused by all the other stations because it showed a greedy, belching pig rising from a map of America – an image too near the truth for the business community to tolerate: 'Freedom' for the 'haves' to keep the 'have-nots' ignorant!

At this point I am only saying that progress is difficult both to define and to achieve. Now, at the end of the twentieth century, I am not expressing the disappointments of an old man. My own life has been fulfilled beyond any of my earlier expectations. I am simply astounded by the extreme depths and heights to which mankind has ventured and the amazing acceleration of changes both for the better and for the worse. We are now entering a period of great uncertainty. This is sad, perhaps, but it can also be interesting and exciting for those who want to try to get to grips with a new realisation of the human condition and then to act accordingly.

To take another example, consider the comparative contributions of nature and nurture in determining what we are. First of all we are a product of our one hundred thousand genes unfolding a blueprint of every aspect of ourselves. Everybody can appreciate that my gender has been genetically determined. I am not bald because neither my father nor grandfather was bald. Not so obviously, I have certain mental and emotional traits which, on further examination, must have been inherited also. An even more interesting characteristic is my behaviour. As Helena Cronin has said, in *A Matter of Life and Death*: 'The clue to understanding our behaviour is to understand the rules of natural selection as laid down by our brains.'

However, our personal identities, aspirations and achievements vitally depend on our experiences. No two people have the same set of experiences, so the possibility of cloning will produce 'lookalikes' with quite different characters, that is, they will be quite distinct and unique people.

I am not a social Darwinist. There is no predestination. The crucial issue, in my humble opinion, is that we are born 'unfinished' with a tremendous capacity to learn. Our genetic code gives us the potential to react in very complex ways to everything and everybody around us. From this, we construct our own particular identity out of the interaction of a multiplicity of factors; but how few people realise their full potential? How many go through life on 'automatic'?

Another interesting point is that there is a mismatch between what our genes were designed to do in the days of palaeolithic man, and what our sophisticated social environment demands of us today, as we sit, imagine a hereafter, watch television and eat junk food instead of hunting, gathering and fighting for mere survival.

I am, therefore, a product of the whole of my life history since conception and it is exceedingly difficult to tease out which characteristic is due solely to my genes and which to an environmental impact. We do not resemble cabbages growing up passively in a field. We are able to take initiatives and influence others as we are influenced by them, but many people leave it to 'them' to decide how the community is organised. They may also see politicians as seeking power merely on their own behalf and being corrupted in the process. I viewed the world differently but I know that I abrogated my own responsibility in not seeking a career in politics. My first love was education, but I was not a mere 'voyeur' of the political scene. I was involved as a 'back-room boy' in the machines that wielded influence in the hope that I could help move things in a direction that would help working people and their families. The grand project of socialism may have been put on the back burner or dropped altogether by most of its protagonists, but I am satisfied that, on balance, there was a constructive outcome to my deliberations – but that is a very subjective judgement.

From the days of my active service in the Atlantic convoys during the war to my retiral as organiser of the Edinburgh Peace Festivals fifty years later, I was engaged in various peace movements and that is a cause of great satisfaction – but not complacency. I believe that these concerted efforts by a great many people were instrumental in preventing an East–West conflict and made it difficult, for example, for the pro-nuclear lobby to sell the 'first-strike' policy.

The following chapters tell the story of my life, describing what I remember of my personal and political thoughts and activities. Hitherto, the personal and the political have rarely been brought together as two sides of the same coin. They are usually pigeonholed quite separately. One has only to look at television programmes or books on the shelves of any library to see what I mean. The two topics are dealt with as being mutually exclusive, and most people drift through life in a cocoon which is only motivated by their personal needs. It seems to me, however, that we can only live a full life if we engage our personal demands within a social and political context. Indeed, I have found that life is much more interesting, understandable and satisfying if we know we belong to one another and act accordingly. This is not altruism. It is in our long-term self-interest.

Although my emotions and feelings have been deep and intense as an individual, invariably my thoughts have been social and my actions political. I have been concerned about the community of interest we have as human beings, in the family, as one of a crew or academic department, and through to the more obvious common concerns of organisations. I deemed the decision-making by these groups as political with a small 'p', not to be confused with 'party political' as the vehicle to obtain real power.

In this regard let us look at what I mean by security. It is felt very deeply by some and at the back of the mind by most, whether in the street, at home or in the workplace. People are made to think that it is only a personal problem as exemplified and reinforced by the ideology behind the TV soap 'Coronation Street' which, in its many hundreds of episodes, has never referred to any social dimension, let alone to trades unions or political movements, even when there is an illegal sacking of workers or criminal activity. In contrast, security as a political issue is then discussed by the authoritative voices of the well-kent faces, as the Scots would say of well-known people, of those in power and in the media, as though it were merely a party political football to be kicked around by 'those who understand such affairs'.

However, many of the commentators of the social and political scene are now generally agreed that the current emphasis on individualism and market forces as the prime movers in society has devalued the idea of John Donne's 'No man is an island' and enhanced Margaret Thatcher's famous remark, over three centuries later, that 'There is no such thing as society'. This sponsorship of the selfish gene has, in my opinion, led to increased cynicism, a lack of respect and trust in one's fellow human beings and, in turn, to the fragmentation of society, an increase in confrontation, divorce, crime, poverty and drugs; indeed, it had led to the alienation of the individual from a coherent view of a supportive system around him and to a big increase in the feeling of insecurity.

Are we, then, becoming a nation of ignorant slobs, victims of media and advertising hype, unwilling to serve anyone but ourselves? Young people boast that 'What matters in life is to look after number one', but even if it can be argued that most people avoid the responsibility of leadership, the social animal in man cannot be suppressed and will flourish in the right political environment.

That, in a nutshell, is why I think that the personal is political but, of course, life is far more complicated than that. Our personal identity and self-worth are shaped by others. We are biologically autonomous but as social beings we need to co-operate within cohesive groups. If we cannot participate we cannot function properly and everybody suffers.

I think Nicola Baker got it right when she wrote in the *New Statesman* (1996) that, 'Only when trouble starts, arguments arise, resentments form and trust is broken do we become conscious of the presence or absence of that invisible glue – social cohesion.' It seems to me, therefore, that we operate within man-made, and not heaven-made, value systems and that our lifestyle depends on our place within these frames of reference just as our opinion of other road users depends on whether we are in the street as a pedestrian, a car driver, a cyclist or a bus passenger. We can change this role several times a day, and amusingly express different opinions, but we don't have much chance to change our social class, race, gender, religion, occupation or age!

Admittedly, these comments don't prove anything. They only serve to indicate that I habitually connect personal problems with the social and political. Most people don't, so what is it in my life that has determined this?

The converse is common knowledge: the political is made personal by those seeking power; otherwise they

Top left: With Robert and John in front of our birthplace, 1980.
Top right: At home with Sybil, 1939.
Bottom: My primary school sixty years later.

Top left: February, 1948.
Top right: West Africa, 1945.
Bottom left: West Africa, 1946.
Bottom left: With Sybil, Southport, 1947.

Top: With Mary, Pamela, Sandra and John, Caterham, 1960.
Bottom: The family at my M.Ed. graduation, Aberdeen, 1967.

Top: With Gisèle at our wedding day party at the Aberdeen Trades Council Social Club, 1971.
Bottom: Our new apartment, Hyères, on the French Riviera, 1979.

would find themselves isolated from their constituents. Nowadays they use deep psychological studies of individuals in many small focus groups in which representative samples of the population are confronted with a variety of problems. Not merely what they say, but also their behaviour and body language are closely watched and analysed. Using this information, political parties then spend millions on the appropriate slogans, sound bites and adverts to shape public opinion in order to achieve an elected dictatorship to further their interests.

The left has been slow in realising the significance of these and other psychological techniques. In the past we have given too much credence to abstract notions of what we would like human beings to be, rather than what they are.

Again, as Nicola Baker explains, 'Today we are reaping the relational consequences of our exclusive focus upon economic priorities in the past two decades. We must redress the balance, challenging the value-base of both left and right. The left's preoccupation with individual rights and economic justice rides uneasily against the focus on family and neighbourhood.'

Subsequent chapters may show that I have walked the tightrope with an uneasy balance between the political and personal demands of the moment, but my convictions have led me to accept the dilemmas. My deep involvement may have been at the expense of my personal relationships and I can understand my family and friends subscribing to that. I tried to follow what I thought was for the greatest good, but you are at liberty to point out that the road to hell is paved with good intentions.

So, some of us, who have led such busy lives that we have not had 'time to stand and stare' now question everything. Until I was early retired these doubts were rhetorical, but then a number of influences coincided. I was approaching the end of my working life against a background of fast-moving global and national events. At the same time, I was able to pay more attention to more personal and leisure options that were opening up in front of me.

For a short period I taught English as a foreign language in a college for telecoms students in the south of France. My favourite text book was *Starting Out* (by Coles and Lord), which amusingly told the story of a teenager, Arthur Newton. They seemed to mimic my own recollections, as though our names were more than mere coincidence.

The story of Arthur Newton.

These tales were woven around a wide variety of situations in which this amiable character tried to do his best, but he lacked social skills and was awkward, confused and often unhappy. Why did he always seem to trip up at the last moment of every episode? Why was he so naive? In any case, why focus only on his personal problems and never on the social and political? Of course, this is the norm so why expect more? Everybody has problems, so make him out to be a problem teenager and we'll laugh at his *faux pas*. We'll feel better for it under the illusion that it's just his bad luck and not ours. The students loved it and fell over themselves trying to find the words, grammar, and intonation necessary to express their opinions in English.

'This record's for Arthur and Mary.'

Arthur's Dream.

Take, for example, Arthur's dream of driving away in a car with Mary, the assistant librarian. The sun is shining as they lie on the beach listening to the radio, which is playing his request record – dedicated to Mary, of course!

But suddenly – PANIC! There's a little girl drowning. Arthur rushes into the sea, pulls her out and places the child in the grateful arms of the mother. He's a hero. He's wonderful. Mary is ecstatic. The whole world's his oyster.

Then Arthur wakes up and reality hits him where it hurts. Life becomes difficult, full of disappointments. He seems to be surrounded by hostility and his friends melt away. His self-esteem is shattered.

Arthur cuts a rather comic figure and we are meant to feel sorry for him. I empathised with his problems, and my students certainly noted that we had the same name and jokingly asked if we were related! Reflecting on our mutual interest in this guy, but for very different reasons, the students were learning English whereas I was teaching it, I posed a series of questions about Arthur and his lifestyle, projecting them into the future.

How does he overcome his inferiority complex? How and why does he become a highly motivated individual? What drives him? In other words, what makes him tick?

I then realised that I was asking the same questions of myself. Why did I act and react in certain ways at various stages in my life? What was the origin of the attitudes I took, especially those concerning social justice and violence? In what ways am I different now at seventy from when I was seven? Who were the greatest influences in my life: my parents? siblings? peer group? teachers or famous personalities? How and when did I engage in politics? Ah! There's the rub. I actually took a very different path from that of Arthur who was only concerned with his job, his pleasures and his encounters with girls and friends. I suspect he could have been interested, as I was, in many social and political problems, but the writer followed the well-trodden path of exclusion.

Putting the spotlight on different periods of one's life can be revealing. Can I finally get to know myself? But just as it is impossible to understand the single frame of a film, pictured outside a cinema, without knowing what went before and after, so too have we got to go back in time and follow it through if we are to understand something of ourselves and the society in which we live.

Autobiographies are notably selective and most of them pretend the truth in an attempt to justify some honour that may have been bestowed on the individual. This would have been only one aspect of their lives and probably the reason for writing it up but, then, this reputation is made to cover all the other aspects. Many, indeed, seem to be on an ego trip and, unwittingly or not, omit the failures, weaknesses and errors of judgement that would help us understand that person in all his fullness.

This, then, is not the usual autobiography. It was intended originally for my grandchildren, family and friends but has evolved into a 'cradle to the grave' story and, to a large extent, mirrors a 'people's story' of Britain in the twentieth century. It may then be of interest to a wider public as a case study of the social history of a typical man – a left-wing activist.

Chapter II
The Thirties in Lancashire

> Children are the living messages we send to a
> time we will not see.
>
> Neil Postman
> *The Disappearance of Childhood*

I was named Raymond Garbet Newton after I was born
into a working-class part of Southport on February 21st,
1927. There was a total eclipse of the sun shortly after and
its path would not pass over the town for another
seventy-two years when other shadows might eclipse my
life. I got my strange middle name from my paternal
grandmother who had died of cancer in 1924, also the year
when my sister, Sybil Frances Mary, had been born.
Eighteen months later my twin brothers, John Brian and
Robert Bernard, appeared on the scene, so I feel as though I
started life as only one of a family and not necessarily an
important part – the typical middle child syndrome.

If the truth be known, my real beginnings were written
in my genes well before this date, handed down from
generation to generation so that the blue colour of my eyes,
my blood group, temperament, susceptibility or resistance
to disease might have been inferred from a study of the
DNA of my ancestors. It is always surprising, however, to

find that cultural inheritance mutates less than the genetic, as instanced by a person's religion and language. So really the whole of history can be implicated!

Grandmother Garbet.

From what I knew, I had only one living grandparent, my father's father, John Harry Newton, who lodged with the family. J.H. had been disinherited when his pub-owning father had left everything to his third wife, Charlotte, when he died in 1901.

I remember my grandfather tapping away on his typewriter in his room upstairs. It had a string with a weight at the end of the table pulling the carriage back when he got to the end of the line. It worked, so he never had it repaired, following the well-known adage, 'If it ain't broke, don't mend it'. My abiding interest was not in his writing but in the scrap paper as he rewrote the script, the reverse side of which I would use as drawing paper. My grandfather used to go out on his sturdy Humber bike to paint nearby landscapes in water-colour or to visit his club in town to play cards, so he was heard rather than seen, talked about rather than talked to.

Grandfather Newton.

My parents met in Liverpool and lived in a flat there until 1924 when they moved to Southport. My father, Bob, left school at fourteen, unqualified to do anything and was eventually called up into the army towards the end of the First World War, then called the Great War, and served in the occupying force in Germany after it. He then picked up a job as office boy with a shipping company. My mother, Alice, didn't get on with her parents; she was five years older than her husband and had had little schooling, mainly because she had been hospitalised with rheumatic fever for two years. However, she managed to leave home at fourteen by staying with her married sister and was found to be good at the jobs she undertook. Alice used to boast that by inventing her age she became an inspector of munitions during the war, but she was thrown out of work when 'the boys came home'.

She was cut off by her parents in Darlington, having rejected their attempts to control every aspect of her life under the banner of Roman Catholicism and conservative values. Her two uncles had been killed in the war and she was told that it was God's will to defend king and country. There was unemployment, poverty and civil strife, especially in Liverpool, where even the police were on strike and the army had been drafted in. All this in a land she was told was 'fit for heroes to live in' yet, as a woman, she was not entitled to vote. That made her think! So the struggle to get a home together and the blatant injustices meted out to otherwise honest and hardworking individuals made it a political household, full of purposeful activity and conversation.

128 Bedford Road was a semi-detached redbrick and slate-roofed house built in 1900 with two storeys, a small garden and outhouses consisting of a coal cellar, wash-house with copper boiler and chimney, together with a dry toilet. In the living room was a bare, pinewood table

that had been scrubbed clean by generations. The springs in the settee no longer supported any weight and at the side was the ever-present sewing basket as the darning of socks and the mending of patches was a daily chore for my mother. The iron kitchen range incorporated an oven with portable steel shelves which we used to heat the beds at night. On the mantelpiece was half a crown in case we had to call Dr Ballantyne by running to his surgery, half a mile down Liverpool Road. Hanging from pulley blocks on the ceiling was a rack for drying clothes. The beds upstairs creaked and groaned and we all shared the same chest of drawers. I don't remember any wardrobes. Our Sunday suits were hung on the oak hallstand. The only furniture that a pawnbroker would have been interested in was in the front room, with its mahogany piano and the bookcase housing a set of Waverley Books of Knowledge and a tea service that came out for visitors. The room was used only then, or at Christmas when a coal fire was lit and the presents opened.

There was, then, an exact date and place on my birth certificate, but no precise beginning to my function as a human being, no *tabula rasa*, no point zero, only a process of development interacting with other processes. The resulting form we call an individual, with an observable identity that we can describe but rarely understand. There are many times when we think we have cracked the nut only to discover a kernel which becomes more complicated as we try to peel off one layer after another until we realise it's a tear-jerking onion and we've bitten off more than we want to chew.

Like all toddlers I must have interacted at every waking moment with everything and everybody around me. The very young human brain is one of great potential as it is only partially wired up, unlike the ready-made computers housed in lower life-forms. The millions of signals flowing into the sense receptors are filtered according to some internal value system. The resulting neural connections form patterns and structures possessed of meaning enabling me, for example, to develop a strategy of living. We now know that these early memories combine to produce a representational model of the world around us with which further inputs are compared and decisions made.

That real world is the same for all, but the individual models of it are different because our experiences of it are different, that is, we become selective. The wonder is, not that inconsistencies and confusions often occur, but that so much consensus is derived from apparent chaos.

I was late in talking, but then went straight into sentences. Was this a question of late development or was I keeping my thoughts to myself until I could contain them no longer? They then burst through the inhibitions like milk suddenly boiling over, producing the occasional tantrum. Whilst it is true that some animals communicate, language is a uniquely human attribute leading to a heightened imagination and consciousness that makes even identical twins like my brothers quite distinctive as individuals.

In retrospect, I must have been negatively affected by experiences before the age of two. My mother was pregnant again before I could walk. She was also unwell and spent long periods in hospital. Identical twins were born prematurely and post-natal care, advice and the material wherewithal were at a minimum. My father left early and returned late from his work in Liverpool. Having renounced Roman Catholicism and been forced to abandon her family, my mother called on my unmarried paternal aunts to give a hand, but they had their own lives to lead and, in addition, there was an active four year old sister demanding attention. My grandfather looked after himself and kept to himself. He came and he went. He wrote boys' stories for a living but he didn't tell any to us.

Throughout these formative years, I have no recollection of people being close to one another, whether physically or otherwise. No one held hands, hugged or kissed, either within or outside the family. Adults meeting for the first time would shake hands. That was all. After that it was just an unemotional 'Hello'. This was so typical amongst the English of the time that its significance is never addressed. Some would argue that it is the vibes that flow from one individual to the next that develop relationships rather than placing emphasis on the more overt mannerisms. Those who have studied other human societies, as well as those of the apes, conclude that a lack of physical contact results in emotional deprivation. Was I helped or hindered at the time?

Who is a reliable witness to all this? Evidence is distorted by hindsight, partial knowledge and wishful thinking, as any judge will tell you. I am less than certain about my first memories. Maybe the images were painted by others commenting on my earlier years. There is also the problem of 'false memory syndrome' although it is undoubtedly true that these perceptions, whether true or false, were used by me to interpret and manipulate the social scene around me. I remember, for example, waiting on my own for what seemed an interminable length of time at the hospital gates, on what seemed to be a huge flight of steps, when I was only two, or was it three, or was it merely a few minutes and only a few steps, and was I really left alone? Unfortunately, it is not reality but our perceptions of reality that mould our attitudes and values, and therefore our decisions. How many of us will admit that our memory may be conveniently playing tricks on us and that we may be seeing and remembering only what we want to see and remember?

128 Bedford Road.

I remember my pre-school years in terms of a secure family background and a somewhat hostile world outside. Anything that moved seemed to interest me, but much the same can be said of a cat! People didn't always appear friendly. What made me into a rather serious character I shall never know. It would be a fruitless exercise to try and ascribe some traits to nature and others to nurture or to start ascribing a proportion to each. What is important is that the die is cast early. As the Jesuits used to say, 'Give me a child until he is seven', etc. The pre-school years made me what I was and am. The subsequent school years merely put flesh on the bones.

So, at five, the film of my life begins in detail, vivid in its colour. On that first day at school I was sitting at a desk near the front and gazing at the alphabet pictures on the wall – A is for Apple to Z is for Zebra – yet I was not supposed to be able to read! Birkdale Infant School was a single-storey building of red brick with a slate roof. The windows were high up and even the teachers couldn't see through them unless they stood on chairs. The toilets were outside, across the asphalt playground, with the larger building of the junior school next door. The head teacher, Miss Mitchell, MA, was a kindly old lady with a Scottish accent. She may only have been about thirty, but to young children everybody older than their parents seems very old indeed.

Drawing, counting, dancing, listening to stories and looking at pictures suddenly made my life interesting. My mind was full of images and symbols and I liked doing things like putting peas between the blotting paper and the sides of the jar, keeping it wet and watching the daily progress of the root and the shoot. I remember seeing the glistening new penny coins marked 1933 and thinking what a long year 1932 had been, the seasons had taken so long to change. Like carbon-14 dating this acts as a good reference point. A year later I was convinced by my classmates that Father Christmas was really my father at Christmas, but I called up the chimney on Christmas Eve just in case, and the analogy with those atheists on their deathbeds praying to go to heaven has not gone amiss. Streets were only lit by gas lamps and activated by a mechanism wound up once a week by a man carrying a ladder to each one in turn. He also altered the timing, but as dusk approached we would kick the lampposts and they would light up just before they were due.

I also remember being told about the Italian invasion of Abyssinia, the Japanese in China and Hitler coming to power in 1933 when I was only five. The neighbours told my mother that it was pretty useless telling children that sort of thing, but these remarks stuck with me and I wanted to know more. Where was Germany? What did the Japanese look like? Were the Italians always cruel?

Calling up the chimney at the age of six to tell Father Christmas what I wanted. It worked, therefore he exists!

I remember coming out of a shop in Chapel Street with my mother talking about the horrors of the 'Great War' as it was then called. Husbands of two of her sisters never came back. I imagined all sorts of scenarios and wondered about my own survival and whether we would be involved in yet another war.

Interestingly, these feelings were replaced in my teens by those of immortality – the norm for boys and young men who then engaged in dangerous activities as though death only happens to others. This is, of course, a sign of immaturity, but it is surprising that well-educated adults who know that man has invented gods and not the other way round, don't make a connection to a leaf rotting underneath a tree, and then conclude that we shall also disappear in the recycling process, together with our minds and souls. We always seem desperately keen to delude ourselves. Of course, the tragedy of human existence is that we know of our own demise and we don't like it. No

doubt wishful thinking about immortality is a necessary prop for some people, but it doesn't make it true.

There was no radio in the house but some 'rich' people had them like the Lewises on the corner. You could tell because they had a long aerial attached to a high post at the bottom of their garden. There were newspapers but not many people bought them and they were in demand to light fires or wrap up chips to keep them hot.

Unlike the other people in the street my parents went to political meetings and visitors to the house talked about the headline news and what was happening to the unemployed. I remember the 1935 general election and a candidate called Carrington. The kids at school had screwed up rolls of newspaper on long pieces of string which they swung round over their heads and into the faces of anybody who was going to vote Labour, so I kept my trap shut. These were working-class children, but they lived in an area devoid of working-class solidarity, unlike the mining and industrial communities. Southport was a seaside resort with seasonal labour, mainly servicing, and was a safe Tory seat. The executives commuting to Liverpool and Manchester were looked on as their betters – a different class of people. Being Protestant and royalist seemed to be the natural order of things and the children were happy if they were given bread and taken to circuses. I was very conscious that my parents were trying to change things and that evil triumphs if good people do nothing, so I grew up with a sense of purpose in a challenging atmosphere that the future was all to play for on the basis of making two steps forward for every one we were pushed back.

At infant school I found life fairly straightforward. Skipping was easy and I couldn't understand why some other children could only hop and walk. Reading was no problem. Tables were memorised. Drawing and making raffia mats was enjoyable. In junior school it dawned on me that I wasn't entirely stupid, especially compared with some classmates who bullied me in the playground. I avoided fights and was called 'cowardly, cowardly custard'. I was also teased about my

middle name, Garbet. There were no real arguments, only rivalry, challenges and dares, so I used to clear off home to play rounders in the street with Ralph Keeley and a few others, interrupted every quarter of an hour by a car or a Ribble bus passing by. I conformed to the yearly round of marbles, conkers, cigarette card collection and swapping. In addition I was good at making peepshows out of a shoe box and cut-out pictures which others could have a look at in exchange for a card, a marble or a sweet. Looking back, it was amazing the number of different activities we engaged in at no cost to anybody.

A typical evening in the Newton household.
Only the living room was heated.

It was 1936 and the Great Depression was ending. At least that was what the Government and the press were saying at the time, but my father was thrown out of work when the firm went into liquidation. At first, talk in the family was about alternative employment, even drawing us all into the conversation to provide a melting pot of suggestions. No doubt this was a ploy to shield us from the truth. There was no other job and Dad became more depressed as the weeks and then the months went by. My father was then seen on the Birkdale and Ainsdale golf courses as a caddie; some days lucky, some days not.

On one occasion, at the time of the Ryder Cup, I went with him to hand out leaflets from the club to the masses of spectators and, knowing it was for the household purse, never sought any reward except for the delight of being in the fresh air. This was the only time I had been taken off school, and I felt guilty that my mother had to write an absence note that was a blatant lie. It threw into relief the question: to what extent does the end justify the means? Perhaps I felt guilty of the eleventh commandment, 'Thou shalt not be found out'.

1936 and subsequent years remained vivid in my memory; helping Mum collect for 'Milk for Spain' when the Spanish Civil War was front-page news, together with pictures of the

Queen's new hat. We also went to the Co-op field days where there were bags of buns, three-legged races and bands playing. At one in particular mother spoke through

the public address system and showed me a different side to her character, a confident and persuasive speaker.

Up till then there were separate men's and women's guilds. My parents founded the Mixed Guild, mother as president and father as secretary, and this was the reason that a typewriter and a table of correspondence permanently occupied a corner of the sitting room. In the summer of 1937 mother went to the Soviet Union as the Lancashire representative of the Co-op guilds, and was then invited to speak all over the county to talk about it. I was secretly proud of her new-found importance, but I was reticent in my own comments to friends as it was not the received wisdom of the moment and I was caught between being thought of as 'odd' and my desire to be identified as typical of my peer group. However, it did establish in my mind that my parents' contribution to the work of organisations added value to their worth and it never occurred to me that it also meant less time devoted to us children. We all seemed free to do our own thing and that became the norm.

One day, as my brothers and I were walking past the Unitarian church, an elderly lady told us about Thursday evenings there for young people. It was similar to the cubs and scouts but less hierarchical and with a different agenda. The company was mixed in age and gender and the following year I went with them, my first time away from home, to a camp that the church had organised at Embsay, near Skipton. I was used to the fresh air and the rain, but coming from an area where the whole sky reached down to a flat landscape as far as the eye could see I stood in awe of the great limestone gorge of Gordale, the rushing streams and the Strid of Bolton Abbey and the smell of sausages from the camp fire. The unique landscape features of the

Carboniferous limestone were imprinted on my memory, and in subsequent decades the Yorkshire Dales were to become my favourite area for geographical fieldwork.

Sundays were occupied with singing in the choir at St Peter's for a small annual sum and a day out to Blackpool or New Brighton. I enjoyed the singing but I wondered at the way adults imprisoned themselves in dogma, superstition, ritual and hypocrisy. Obviously, my home 'education' was stronger than that from outside, but I lacked the confidence to argue my case, so I played along with the system but refused to go to the communion classes. Instead I preferred to play in the street.

In general, I found it easier to be conventional in some things in order to admit that I was a labour supporter. My parents were actually in the Left Book Club and members of the Communist Party of Great Britain (CPGB). Because Dad was out of work he used to collect copies of the *Daily Worker* from Chapel Street Station each morning. The wholesalers wouldn't handle them and occasionally the bundle was found on the railway lines, thrown there by the very workers they were trying to help. Accompanying my dad probably gave me more political education than any number of lectures.

I also read the leaflets that Dad gave me to distribute round the houses so I became well versed in campaigning in the 'struggle for socialism'. At that time priority was given in the movement to the threat from the rise of Fascism in Europe and the 'neutral' policy of the British Government allowing Franco, Hitler and Mussolini to expand their territory and power. The policy of 'non-intervention' in Spain was, in fact, tacit support for Franco. There was more overt support for Hitler and Mussolini to ban trades unions and arrest the communists, at least by the *Daily Mail*, which seemed at the time to have been given an undeserved status like *The Times*.

Now, sixty years on, a former member of the International Brigade, Steve Fullerton, told us in Edinburgh how he had lost many of his comrades in Spain. He returned after that war had ended to join the RAF to participate throughout the Second World War. He then joined the civil service but after several years MI5 investigators told the authorities of his Spanish experience. He was sacked and banned from all government employment only for this reason. With a glint in his eye he said, 'I could have saved the Government a lot of money investigating if only they had asked me, as I was as proud of it then as now.' Bob Cooney was another International Brigader I got to know well when he returned to Aberdeen after a lifetime of anti-fascist struggle and consequent victimisation by employers circulating a blacklist.

It has been my privilege to have been associated with many such people who were so principled and courageous yet modest and unassuming. I could do a lot of name-dropping of well-kent faces, as they say in Scotland, that I have met over the years, such as Yasser Arafat in Berlin, Sir Malcolm Rifkind at a Peace Festival Meeting he addressed, President Ortega of Nicaragua when the Lord Provost introduced me to him in the Edinburgh City Chambers, Annie Lennox on a family visit to Aberdeen, the

Queen at her garden party at Holyrood, and over a period of time Sheena Macdonald, Mick McGahey and so on, but I am not tempted into stories that have had little influence over my life. It is unfortunate that the hundred and one individuals who have influenced me most have not been exceptional, but have been, and still are, nevertheless, typical of those engaged in solid day-to-day activity and thought for the welfare of their fellow-beings. It is their experiences, attitudes and interests, rather than those of the 'big names' that have maintained my faith in the human race.

It was my parents, especially my mother, who were the key influences, directing my attention to what was happening in the rest of the world. Never a day passed without their comments on global and national affairs, and this seemed to be at variance with what was happening in other families. Therefore, we seemed to be swimming against the tide of conventional wisdom, and to that extent life was difficult.

However, by the same measure, I felt rather special to be associated with this purposeful discussion and activity. These two sides of the coin were elegantly expressed by the feature writer, Martin Kettle, of *The Guardian*, June 14th, 1997, when he concluded at the end of his analysis of *Growing up as a Red*: 'I think that the children of communists have gone through something enviable. Not enough people on the left have had to grapple with the facts of the socialist century. Most of the children of communists of my acquaintance believe that there are no easy answers but that there are questions which must not be avoided either.'

Reverting back to my primary school days, I felt privileged to be involved in these 'grown-up' activities, especially as my siblings didn't seem to have been given such 'responsibilities' but most of my leisure time was taken up out of doors roaming the links, the dune-lined beach, blackberrying on the golf courses, watching others at the fairground, especially on the water chute and Noah's ark.

With my twin brothers I built dams across the ebbing tide, learnt to swim in Ainsdale Lake, made model boats out of pieces of wood, cork and paper with a few tacks and nails and sailed them on the pond built for that purpose. I wasn't at all envious of the boys looking bored as their fathers pushed out their pricey-looking boats and new model yachts. When there was disagreement as to what to do next, the twins stuck together and outvoted me, so I often felt alone but never lonely. Sometimes I felt sad, but not unhappy and I was never bored. I had little respect for classmates who competed to see who could bait the teacher the most, swear and call insults, fight and not cry and tell the dirtiest jokes.

As there was no sex education either at home or at school, I had to try and disentangle the conflicting bits of information and disinformation inherent in some of the jokes and whispered comments. Even at seven it seemed quite illogical to have a male organ for two very different purposes, namely to get rid of liquid waste and to put into females to create a new life. No wonder there was secrecy, confusion, guilt, dirt, fascination as well as doubts wrapped up in this enigma. Boys who told the most bizarre jokes collected the most friends, but my upbringing bordered on the puritanical and I generally kept my distance. This was a slight problem because I would then remain on the periphery of the group without the empowerment that status gives. It now seems to me that independently minded people will always be in a minority. On the other hand, these people must have the humility to respect the popular view for what it is, and this is not always a comfortable line to follow.

Being on the fringes and never at the centre of cliques and gangs, I was also last in line to be chosen in teams such as rounders, football or cricket. Neither did I accept 'dares' that constituted the entry qualification to the particular gang because there was no doubting in my mind of what was right and what was wrong and I said so, getting the reply that I was a sissy. It was undoubtedly the case that the influence of peer group pressure was immeasurably greater than that of the parents and teachers, at least with the boys I knew. Therefore, I began to feel that I was on a minor road increasingly distant from the major one that others wanted to follow.

My dream world was one of kind people but also one of cars, aeroplanes and labour-saving inventions. It tended to be a world of progress and certainty, of class-consciousness and of struggle against the power of a privileged few to exploit the rest. We might have doubts about all of this half a century later, but at that time I did seem to express in my general attitude and behaviour a high moral tone. At the same time my emotions were not well catered for and situations were oversimplified. However, I marked myself off from the other boys who seemed to be driven only by their immediate desires and instincts.

At the age of ten 'real' boys went deliberately into troubled areas like apple-scrumping, kicking an old lady's dog, stoning windows or knocking on doors and running off, pulling girls' knickers down and threatening them not to tell, shouting insults at disabled people and especially those with Down's syndrome, nicking an orange from the greengrocers and bragging about it. 'I pinched two' would retort the next lad whether or not he had done.

It is difficult enough for adults, let alone children, not to follow the crowd. As Nietzsche said, 'Madness is rare in individuals but in groups, parties and nations it is the rule.' It began to dawn on me that any dialogue within a group becomes poisoned with slogans and the obvious is rarely questioned.

I was not without my own contradictions: sociable but a loner, practical yet idealist, inhibited but unrestrainable, co-operative and competitive, streetwise yet naive.

My leg was easily pulled and when we queued for the dentist on his annual visit to the school, the boys said they would take out my teeth there and then with a huge pair of pliers, so I began to blubber as soon as my name was called. It was some ten years on before I went without qualms to the dentist, by which time my teeth were in a bad state and needed a dozen visits to get them right, albeit temporarily. On the other hand I remember the happier occasions of my ninth birthday party and my first kiss to Paula Eccles in postman's knock and the big Christmas party in the town hall for the children of the unemployed.

Mine was a very nuclear family whose only extension seemed to comprise two cousins, Frank and Gerald, who very occasionally called in with their parents on a Sunday visit to the seaside from Nelson, when mother would reach to the top of the store cupboard for a tin of Del Monte peaches and one of Fussell's thick cream.

In 1937 we accompanied my dad to Bertram Mills circus, held in a field on the other side of town in Preston New Road. It was my first circus with plenty of performing animals. I came away whistling the theme tune which remains with me as evocative and nostalgic but now hated as I recall the words – 'Land of Hope and Glory'. In March of 1938 I cycled with my dad to the Grand National at Aintree and stood for half an hour at the Canal Turn waiting for the rush of galloping horses and ten minutes later for the second time round the circuit. These were exceptions. We were normally doing what we wanted and with whom we wanted.

Where were the parents in those days? No child was accompanied to school, to the pictures, to the park or indeed anywhere except to visit relations. The peer group was everything – and we felt safe.

Children could be cruel to other children, but they rarely felt insecure as their extended family was not far away. Comics were swapped, bartering went on for bats, balls and hoops but these were specifically boys' activities. Girls had dolls and played nurses or hopscotch. Indeed, where was my sister? She seemed always to be out with her friends. In addition, she went to a church school, St Philip's, somewhat further away, and then won a scholarship to the girls' high school. Our mother insisted to the neighbours that it was more important to educate a girl on the basis that it would not only give her a career and the possibility of economic independence, but also because it was women who educate the next generation. The neighbours didn't seem to agree but it registered with me that girls had problems that boys didn't have.

From what has been said it would appear that I spent a lot of my spare time roaming the golf links or giving out leaflets with my dad. This was not the case. I liked school and my parents encouraged me to take an interest, though they never visited nor spoke to the teachers. However, there was always the topic of getting qualifications and a job in some profession or other. To get on meant getting out. To get out meant getting on, but they were largely ignorant of the intricacies of the educational ladder.

In January 1938 the crunch came for me in the last year of junior school in the form of the eleven plus exam. The school never provided any homework and I avoided doing the sums from an old arithmetic textbook that my parents had picked up from somewhere. I didn't like it and I didn't do any of it. On the Saturday morning of the exam, I turned up but my friend Ralph didn't. His parents didn't want him to be 'stuck up' and grow away from the family. In any case, parents had to agree to allow their child to stay on after the leaving age of fourteen to take the matric and this seemed a big commitment to undertake years in advance. Of course, those familiar with the system knew that there was no legal obligation and any excuse would have done if the occasion arose. To cut a long story short, I failed the eleven plus. Only one boy passed, one Robert Moore, and the teachers congratulated him and each other that the school had got somebody through.

However, it was possible then to pay to go to the grammar school and some professional friends and comrades rallied round and gave my parents the twelve guineas for the first year's fees. So I went to the grammar school in the autumn of 1938 and this opened doors that were never to be closed. I felt grateful that my mother had gone to so much trouble when I knew I hadn't taken the trouble myself, but I didn't express this to anyone. My mother could have left me to my own devices saying, 'It serves you right for not doing the homework I suggested', but she never did. Of course, we knew, as a family, that we were buying privilege in a system that was adept at throwing a few crumbs to the poor and elevating some of them in order that the rich could perpetuate their power over the rest.

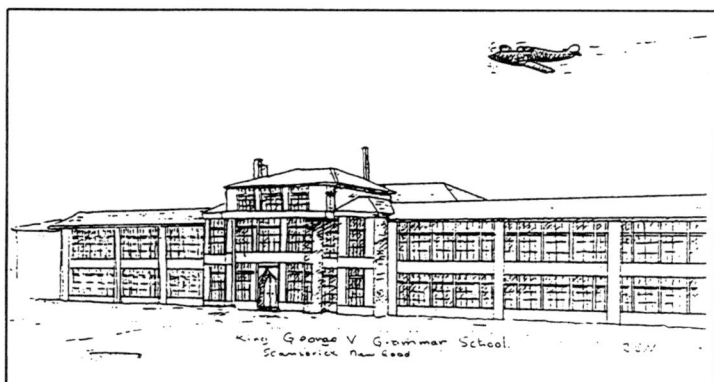

King George V Grammar School. Scunsorick Now Good.

This, then, is my background as a shy and rather serious boy, to some extent a loner, poorly dressed but well fed and healthy, already with a track record in 'the struggle for socialism' and with feelings for the oppressed in an unjust world, gathering a wide range of interests but not being

42

talented in any one, liking the open air but capable of sitting through some indifferent teaching, and, last but not least, I was beginning to be independently minded or stubborn or just determined – the choice is yours!

Chapter III
The Forties at School

> Your children are not your children.
> They are the sons and daughters of Life's
> longing for itself.
> They come through you but not from you,
> And though they are with you yet they belong
> not to you.
>
> Kahlil Gibran
> *The Prophet*

In September 1938 I put on my new school blazer, cap and tie in maroon and black stripes and entered the new world of the King George V Grammar School for Boys situated at the edge of town on Scarisbrick New Road. I had previously walked to primary school. Now I cycled the two miles like most of the other pupils, with school bag on my back and sandwiches in the saddlebag.

Boys wore shorts until they were at least thirteen,

but only the grammar school and private schools had uniforms. This camouflaged differences in wealth and class but a person's accent and dialect located his position in the pecking order of society. Even within the working class there were many levels, discernible with the aid of clues such as address, job, leisure interests and association, just as everybody in Ulster knows who is a Protestant and who is a Catholic.

I rated myself as upper working class, upwardly mobile to the lower part of the middle class as I was now in a very middle class milieu. I admired the self-assured confidence of the fee-paying as against the scholarship boys and found that as one of the former I was given an undeserved social standing and recognition by both pupils and teachers. I was to learn later that the Scots simply do not appreciate the English notion of class and their persistent feeling for an imperial past and the dominant culture that permeates the psyche. The English, for their part, are generally too arrogant to admit it or descend into a self-deprecating mode with the intention of reinforcing the opposite.

One of my first impressions of my new classmates was that of strange names, unfamiliar accents and different religions and denominations. My father was still on the dole but I neither mentioned nor denied this. I was, however, conscious of my limited means to follow my friends into the tuck shop. I was also unable to invite my friends home, but the catchment area of the school was so wide that almost all of my school friends lived some distance away.

Was the school a privileged hothouse to train an elite? Would it warp my proletarian values? Being an all-male environment would it mould my attitude to women as a species apart? Nobody knows. We can only guess.

One thing is certain. It was an excellent academic education. There were now many subject divisions, with a separate schoolmaster for each, and the school prospectus exuded high qualifications and experience. The lessons were well structured with a recap of the previous lesson, oral and written work with regular homework. I knew that I was keeping up with the work but got the biggest surprise of my life when I came fifth out of twenty-eight in the first term's exams. The first five were added to an honours list. To hear my name read out when I had previously been labelled an eleven-plus failure gave me the confidence that was to enable me to be in the honours list every term of my school career. I reached second on one occasion, but never top, a characteristic that was to accompany me all my life. I always judged that to come first meant that I had to give up other interests which I was reluctant to do. I was planning for a long-term future and not immediate status.

What surprised me was the gradual deterioration of the attainment of some of my fellow pupils who had already done some French, Latin and mathematics in prep school, and who were exceedingly articulate and seemingly bright. Was it like the hothouse plants that cannot compete when the others catch up? I never did catch up in English literature, as the concepts and vocabulary were over my head. At one point in the second year I made what I thought was a brave effort to emulate those who seemed so successful at using long words with good effect but I received my homework essay back with the comment, 'You are inebriated with the exuberance of your own verbosity.' Thereafter I kept to the simpler Anglo-Saxon vocabulary.

Geography and the sciences especially interested me, and I was good at maths, French and history. I enjoyed the art club after school, especially devising posters and writing in Gothic script rather than painting landscapes, a skill that my twin brothers accomplished with ease. I was only mediocre in the gym and on the playing field so I used to go instead to the Victoria swimming baths on the promenade, competing eventually for Evans House and the school, as well as gaining the Silver Award of Merit for lifesaving.

In the summer athletics took over and I found that I was best as a middle-distance runner, but all along my goal was the matriculation exams of the Joint Matriculation Board of the Northern Universities, so I didn't let anything else stand in its way. Boys were called only by their surnames as in the public schools, so I recollect very graphically my classmates, and have a photographic memory of their faces, but can't remember their first names! There was Heath with his pictures of American pin-ups, Bridges and his fabulous birthday party, the disabled Parry who lived across the road from the school and had a drum kit which he beat to death from his wheelchair, Ross and his record-breaking one hundred yards freestyle swimming, Barlow the

Londoner who eventually returned there, Amos, Blackburn, Duerden and others who supported me when I led a snowball fight against the marauding seniors.

This was a relatively new school, but like most English grammar schools, it followed the ethos of the public schools except that there was no boarding. It was, of course, a good education because the education authority not only creamed off the best pupils, but also the best teachers. The grammar school was given the lion's share of local authority spending and it gave its 'old boys' a kickstart in any application for a job.

I very much appreciated the luck of being given the opportunity to get a 'real' education, but I also knew that the system was devised to reinforce the belief that only twenty-two per cent of children were capable of following an academic course with seven per cent going on to a higher education course. I was part of a minority of 'winners' on the backs of a majority of losers, 'the undeserving poor', but I hope I never lost sight of my roots. Unlike those who thought of their exclusive and rightful inheritance of the best that society could offer and who occasionally gave a mite to charity to salve their consciences, my thoughts focused on the need to change society to a more caring and sharing one. At the same time I concentrated on jumping the necessary academic hurdles in order to get a satisfying, secure and rewarding job. I accepted that most jobs are so dull, boring and tiring that those who have no other option spend their waking hours dreaming of the pseudo-excitement of winning the pools without the foggiest idea of the problems they would face if they did!

I remember well the Spanish Civil War when the legitimate government had been defeated by Franco with the aid of Hitler and Mussolini. The British battalion had suffered heavy casualties and my parents had discussed with other comrades those who wouldn't be coming back, including a brilliant young philosopher, Christopher Cauldwell, who had just published a seminal work, *Illusion and Reality*. He had driven an ambulance across France to Spain, the result of door-to-door collections in Britain, and was killed in the battle of Jarama.

The shadow of war was covering Europe, but Hitler had declared in *Mein Kampf* that the aim of a stronger Germany was to defeat Bolshevism. That's why he received support from members of the British Government and the aristocracy, but the activists in the Labour movement had warned that Hitler could turn west as well as east – as my mother never ceased telling us.

I read my mother's pamphlet, 'Guilty Men' by Michael Foot, and also Frank Pitcairn's 'Notes' in the *Daily Worker*, especially on the exposures of the Cliveden Set. Pitcairn's real name was Claude Cockburn, whom I was to meet in front of the TV cameras in Aberdeen some thirty years later for the programme *One Pair of Eyes*, when Claude compared the pre-war days of attempts to 'roll-back communism' with the cold war of the time.

I was only twelve when the war broke out, yet I remember the political contexts and events, as described and explained by my mother on an almost daily basis. With hindsight, the analyses were remarkably accurate and poignant, and are etched permanently on my memory.

For example, when Chamberlain came back from a meeting with Hitler in Munich, waving a piece of paper and declaring 'Peace in our time' the press and radio hailed it as a victory for the government. The newsreels on the cinema screens showed the grateful and cheering population, but my mother explained that this was all wrong. It was an attempt, she said, to encourage Hitler to expand eastwards without interference from the west.

It seemed to me that this was also the reason why Britain refused to sign a mutual defence pact with France and the Soviet Union that would attempt to contain Hitler. Instead, the Soviet Union made a non-aggression pact with Germany, not, as is sometimes portrayed, a mutual defence pact, but in order to gain time before the inevitable onslaught. Later, when Hess, Hitler's deputy, parachuted on to Lord Hamilton's estate in Scotland, my mother immediately explained that his mission was to sue for non-intervention by the British as the Germans prepared to attack Russia.

I remember this clearly, as I thought it was rather odd for my mother to have such detailed information that wasn't currently expressed in the news. None of my classmates were privileged enough to have had that analysis, though it is now generally accepted and perhaps enhanced rather than weakened by the Government's decision to keep the list of Hess's contacts top secret, 'in the national interest', beyond the normal fifty year rule. Historians now accept my mother's explanation!

In 1938 rearmament was in full swing. Air-raid shelters of brick, concrete and sandbags were being built at street corners and in the parks. Following the experience of the bombing in Spain there was a campaign for deep shelters as advocated by Professor J.B.S. Haldane in feature articles in the *Daily Worker*, but they were deemed too expensive for the general population.

The extensive sandy beaches at Southport were flecked with posts to inhibit an invasion of landing craft or parachute drops. My mother, reflecting on the shortages during the First World War bought a sack of sugar, a tin of isinglass to preserve eggs, and tins of fruit to put under the larder stairs. War was now being talked about.

I didn't go to the cinema very often but *Professor Mamlock* made a deep impression on me even though I was not quite sure how much of it was fact and how much was fiction. It told the tale of a Jew who refused to leave his house and how the whole family was victimised. After 'Kristalnacht' he was killed by the Storm Troopers as the 'silent majority' merely watched from the sidelines.

With a few others from the Left Book Club, which had a room above a shop in the centre of town, I gave out leaflets as the crowds emerged from the film. It told them of the need to confront fascism and about a popular movement called The People's Convention, reiterating the adage that evil will conquer if good people do nothing.

At one well-attended meeting in the Cambridge Hall a certain black-moustached dockers' leader, Leo McGree from Liverpool, got a rousing reception and a massive collection, not so much for his politics as for his tremendous sense of humour.

How true were the words of Pastor Neimoller who was imprisoned by the Nazis: 'First they came for the communists and I did not speak out because I was not a communist. Then they came for the Jews and I did not speak out because I was not a Jew. Next they came for the trades unionists and I did not speak out because I was not a trade unionist. Then they came for me and there was no one left to speak out for me.'

At 11 a.m. on Sunday, September 3rd, 1939, my twin brothers and myself were singing in the choir at St Peter's when the vicar announced that Britain had declared war on Germany, as agreed with the Poles. This came as no surprise as talk of the war had been in the air for some time.

Armed conflict had already started before Britain entered the war and did not intensify after it was declared. There was a period called the 'Phoney War' because nothing much seemed to happen except for a few ships being sunk. My school friends rarely talked about the war at first, merely parroting newspaper stories about royalty at the races, somebody found murdered, the sports results or the latest Hollywood gossip.

The film *The Great Dictator* was certainly catching people's imagination, mainly because Charlie Chaplin was so funny. But he was also deeply serious and I gave out leaflets, yet again, with Charlie's remarkable speech when, in the film, he replaced Hitler as a lookalike before the massive Nuremberg Rally, telling them that he had been wrong to be so aggressive and that they should now disarm and fight for a better world for the whole of humanity. What a great film, by a great man with a great idea?

So the clouds of war rolled over Britain. The garden rails were taken away for scrap. The 'Dig for Victory' campaign started with demonstration plots replacing the flower beds along the promenade, which inspired me to dig up an allotment on the Moss at Birkdale, just a short bicycle ride away.

The Ministry of Information issued leaflets on everything from preserving fruit to first aid, and from blackout materials to the saving of energy by filling the bath to no more than the regulation four inches. They also gave advice on the growing of vegetables, but having followed the instructions I found that the crops were all ready for harvesting at the same time; a succession was subsequently easily planned but more difficult to organise.

To all those who suffered indescribable misery during the war it may seem incongruous that my family, like many others, suddenly enjoyed a rise in their standard of living and even their quality of life. My father got a job. Money came into the house. Rationing meant not so much a restriction as an invitation to buy a whole range of food and goods that we weren't able to afford before the war. The full rations were bought and Dad sold the bacon to Mr Ball the insurance man who called every Saturday morning.

Like many other working-class people my parents only insured for funerals lest the ignominy of a pauper's grave awaited them. For the first time there was a radio in the house – a cheap brown Bakelite one tuned in for most of the time to the Home Service of the BBC, but sometimes to the Light Programme with Tommy Handley's ITMA, *Workers' Playtime*, *Happidrome* or *Music Hall*. Such programmes certainly brought laughter into the house and there was an added quality of listening together. With a bit of knob twiddling it was possible to hear Lord Haw-Haw's 'Germany calling, Germany calling'. This English traitor gave details of events not broadcast by the BBC, but with plausible comments to establish his credibility, such as details of bombing raids. This would be followed by some opinions of his own with an easy conversational manner and then stone-biting criticism of Britain's war effort which would be a topic of discussion in the playground the following morning.

In any case, the BBC was very much an arm of the Government of the day and only the plummy accents of the public school came over the air in the serious programmes and news items. Regional accents were reserved for comedy, but there was a near revolution of the middle classes when the Yorkshireman Wilfred Pickles was brought in to read the news and the press had a field day.

The *Daily Worker* was banned and other newspapers were censored. *Movietone News* in the cinema was meant to raise morale with a lot of pseudo-patriotic charm. Labour had joined a National Government, but it was Churchill and Boothby who led the debate against Chamberlain's war policies which in turn led to his fall from grace.

Churchill's eloquence over the radio was important in the new prosecution of the war with his promise of 'blood, toil, tears and sweat' and, as a result, the population was given a clearer sense of purpose and direction.

In 1939 I was awarded an internal scholarship, together with another fee-payer, Bryan Wade. That is, no more fees were required, which was just as well for me for that was the extent of the loan that my mother had obtained to send me to the grammar school in the first place. Bryan Wade's father, who was a tall, elegant figure, instructed the ARP Wardens in air-raid protection, especially against gas attacks and firefighting. Everybody had been provided with a gas mask in a cardboard box. Most people made a better carrying case and shoulder strap and it was carried night and day wherever you went. I volunteered to take a weekend course and was told how to paste strips of paper on the window to counteract the effects of flying glass. I had already read about such measures in the leaflets that could be picked up in the libraries and the newly formed community centres, but the practical side was completely new and I got a great deal of satisfaction tackling the burning magnesium of an incendiary device with a long-handled rake and pan. Another exercise was the use of sand and stirrup pumps against fires and finally, with my rubber-faced gas mask with its carbon-filled canister, walking through an air-locked passage of tear gas. Those who hadn't got their gas masks on snug round their face soon knew about it, including big, tough men exiting with their eyes streaming! This was amusing but in a real situation it could have been mustard gas and quite a different story.

In 1940 Bootle High School was evacuated to Southport and they used the school in the afternoons. I found myself in various church halls without any materials or equipment, but the teachers were quite resourceful and they engaged the pupils in more discussion.

On one occasion they got a 'magic lantern' from somewhere and showed some ancient slides. For the first time the class was taken out on nature walks round Kew Pond and the Moss. Southport is built on sand dunes, but a mile or so inland is an extensive area of fen with black peaty soils and a network of drainage ditches, the remains of a post-glacial lake called the Mere. Around the rim used to inhabit the rimmers and the name Rimmer was common in the area.

Houses built on the Moss often subsided as the peat dried out with the lowering of the water table. For the same reason the school developed cracks as though there had been an earthquake and later had to be demolished.

Anyway, these walks round the area may have been imposed due to lack of accommodation in the initial weeks, but they reinforced my attachment to the open air with some specific knowledge about the here and now.

The blackout was rigorously enforced by the wardens knocking on the door if there was even the smallest chink of light. At home in Bedford Road only the living room was regularly used and blacked out. There was usually a coal fire and the back boiler heated the hot water. As this was the only warm room the whole family congregated there. In winter the bedrooms were cold, but a hot plate from the oven was put into the bed for about ten minutes before getting into it. Adding your vest and socks to your pyjamas also helped. This happened to be useful when a landmine dropped nearby, blew in the front windows and we were taken downstairs for the night, wrapped in coats and spare blankets.

Cheap translucent glass replaced the broken panes, but this was the least of the family worries and did not warrant even a discussion the following morning. Of continuing concern was the political situation, but, like most children entering their teens, money was needed for the increasing demand for clothing and leisure, so I found a Saturday job as an errand boy at Hoyles the grocer's.

Everything in the grocer's was packaged by hand using paper bags and bulk supplies, whether sugar, biscuits, dried peas or bacon. The scraps and broken bits were sold cheaply and off-ration and it was common, for example, to have children coming in for a tuppenny bag of broken biscuits, but on Saturdays I got in first with my order, taking it home when I finished at five. As there were rarely biscuits of any sort in the house these were counted as luxuries. I got to know the area and the houses well as I trundled back and forth on my bike and I wondered who was going to tip me at Christmas. To my surprise the correlation between the size or value of the house that I visited and the size of the tip was very low, and the concept of unpredictability was registered. Of course, in some smaller houses there

On my Saturday delivery bike, 1940.

could have been several wage earners, whereas an old-age pensioner might occupy a big house, but I never really disentangled the problem.

In retrospect, the variety of foods was limited but wholesome and, in general, the level of nutrition rose during the war and the population's health was better than before. Spam and dried eggs were introduced. So too was cod liver oil and malt for children. There was a one-third-pint bottle of milk for everybody at school and hot meals available in community centres. Ways of economising and avoiding waste became habits that the 'war generation' carried on for the rest of their lives, and their ways of 'make do and mend' contrast sharply with the disease of consumerism that has infected so much of the more affluent parts of the world today.

During the Liverpool blitz the van driver who delivered the bread from the central bakery told of the previous night's bombing, and how he had spent the night dragging out casualties and fighting the fires as an auxiliary. At this time civilians and merchant seamen were suffering more than those in the forces.

My family were not directly affected but amongst my abiding memories are the ack-ack guns firing and shells exploding in mid-air, the tell-tale 'wow-wow' droning of the German bombers, the searchlights criss-crossing the night sky, the orange glow in the direction of Liverpool and then the ghostly silence after the all-clear had been sounded, followed by an uneasy sleep. Knowledge of bombed sites and wrecked planes were shared between pupils the next day, and some brought souvenirs to prove the point.

My father took his turn at fire-watching in Liverpool and also did a spell assisting the anti-aircraft crews as a member of the Home Guard. One night he had a meeting so he swapped with a colleague. Returning from work the next day he described how a bomb had gone down the lift shaft of the building he was scheduled to fire-watch, demolishing the entire building, so he spent the day helping to set up a temporary office elsewhere.

Everything was so matter of fact. Life went on as usual, but I was at my most impressionable age, so I never found a dull moment. At first when the sirens sounded everybody went to some sort of shelter. At school this was under the Haig Road football stadium that backed on to the school playing field. Some classes had set work to do. Others engaged in community singing, but in subsequent years they carried on working in the classrooms. Women as well as men were called up to do some sort of service – in the forces, in the factories or on the farms. Young people who left school were interviewed and not only found jobs immediately but were questioned about their leisure time to make sure they spent it usefully.

Everybody accepted the difficulties but, of course, there was a common goal and a sense of purpose pervading everyday life. The superficial was differentiated from the meaningful.

Yes, there were black marketeers but no one would have admitted to dealing with them. The tale went round of a driver making a regular visit to a farm to collect 'surplus' eggs, but one day he noticed that the black Riley of a police car was following him. He drove into the hospital so the police carried on!

The popular view of political events closely followed that of the press and the radio, but my mother frequently gave a different interpretation. She called it a 'class analysis' because of the clash of interest between those who worked by hand and brain for a wage and those owned the wealth and were able then to dictate economic policy. The establishment used the media and the state machine to perpetuate their privileged position. Therefore, according to my mother, the working class had got to be organised to defend themselves or they would just be kept down; by the same measure the poor would get poorer and the rich would get richer.

Politics was not, therefore, just a matter of personality clashes, a view beloved by journalists and historians, but of individuals attempting to survive and throwing up social movements in the process.

This made sense to me, even though jargon, sectarianism and dogmatism crept into the arguments, so I joined the Young Communist League which met every Monday evening in the town centre. Sometimes there was a good speaker and a knowledgeable chairperson, but this was not often, and the discussion centred on the most assertive character there, which kept me quiet.

I didn't go to the social events at the weekend as I had my Saturday job and homework to do. I also took things too seriously to listen to old records, have an under-age drink, accept a cigarette or compete with the others for the minority of girls. Girls had been an academic rather than an emotional problem up to then, but now, at the age of thirteen, the hormones of puberty began working so I looked at girls in a different light from even a year earlier. Coming from an all-boys school my eyes were drawn to them, but I had no idea of how to approach them.

Joyce Bates met the boys after choir on a Sunday but I didn't get a look in. Jean Woodall was dating Harry Eccles, a couple of years older, but there was a younger sister, Doris, who was lively, bright, and attractive, with blonde hair and a shapely figure. After a week's thought and planning I went round to her house, rehearsing what I was going to say: 'Will you come to the cinema on Saturday night...? What are you doing tomorrow night...? Do you want to go for a walk...?' The thoughts were endless, but I finally knocked nervously on the front door. Her mother simply said that she was at her boyfriend's house! Crestfallen, I went away without even saying, 'Thanks'.

I rated myself poorly in the dating game. My social skills generally were very weak as I was always afraid of making a *faux pas*. I blushed and was shy yet I lacked neither courage nor willpower to do what I had decided to do whenever action was required.

However, Ted Willis and I met two girls and went out as a foursome. I enjoyed the company of Isobel, who had not long arrived in Southport, sent by her parents in London as the air raids there had increased. When my classmates and friends saw me they greeted me with, 'Is a bell necessary on a bike?'

Isobel and I got as far as holding hands in the cinema, but shortly afterwards she went back to London. By a strange coincidence we met again ten years later. She was as beautiful as ever. Isobel had been a nurse, but was now married to a film director. My bad luck again!

I was now fourteen, coming up fifteen, and I had got a better paid job at Park's Bakery, assisting in a 5cwt. Ford delivery van. Next door to a regular customer was another girl of my dreams. How could I introduce myself? I eventually found out her name as her brother was at the grammar school – not a bad start, but her brother didn't seem to be the kind that would arrange a meeting so I wrote a letter, substituting Arthur for Ray so that her brother wouldn't put a spoke in the wheel. We met, went to Victoria Park, had a hot peppermint drink in Lord Street and went to the Odeon cinema.

I spent all my pocket money but it was worth it as it was at last a complete conquest. We arranged to meet again but as we were about to part I explained that actually my name was Ray, not Arthur. She fell into tears and ran off. I had deceived her, but only a little... but I then realised that the bottom had fallen out of everything I had said until there was no trust left. I reflected on this and vowed that I would henceforth abandon 'hidden agendas' especially where relationships were concerned. Honesty is the best policy, I thought.

I can't claim that it was a matter of high principle, but it was the simplest and easiest option because otherwise I would find myself entangled in an unmanageable superstructure of lies built upon more lies – always the pragmatist! This was my solution; it ought to have been a more principled one.

★

On the morning of June 21st, 1941 the radio announced that Germany had attacked the Soviet Union without warning or declaring war, and along the whole two thousand mile front. My parents went immediately to the local branch secretary of the Communist Party, as they felt that there was a real possibility of Britain standing aside to let them fight it out. This is what Lord Vansittart had advised the government after Hess's flight to Lord Hamilton's estate.

To Churchill's great credit he declared that fascism was the main enemy and therefore Russia would be an ally in that fight. The phoney war had ended. Everyone was galvanised into action by a united labour and trades union movement. Britain was no longer alone and it became possible to imagine the defeat of fascism.

At school, the talk was of the length of time it would take for Russia to surrender. There were various estimates from a few weeks to a few months depending on which commentator or journalist you listened to. A teacher, Mr Williams, opened a discussion on the topic. Some of the pupils said a fortnight, reflecting on the blitzkriegs across the countries of Europe. Others thought it might take up to three months as the distances involved were greater. As I was shaking my head at all these suggestions 'Taffy' asked me to come to the front and give my opinion. I explained why the war game had now changed and that Russia would never surrender.

Mr Williams tried to quell the loud guffaws of disbelief at Nutcase Newton voicing such idiocies. Time went by, six months, then a year. Then the Germans were being pushed back and I gave a wry smile as Mr Williams reminded the class of what was said at the discussion at the end of the summer term in 1941.

There was a campaign for the West to open a second front and both Stalin and Roosevelt talked about the need for this. Churchill, however, procrastinated and went for the so-called 'Soft under-belly of the Axis' in the Mediterranean, with long supply lines and difficult terrain, especially in Italy where my schoolboy friend Ralph Keeley's two brothers, Jim and Jack, were killed. At the time, the news of someone being killed in action was quickly put out of one's mind.

It was only much later that it struck me that I was enjoying an interesting life and that these poor suckers had none of it. In the conference season of 1943 I joined a demonstration for the second front when the news came through of the 'invasion' of Dieppe, but elation soon turned to sadness as it transpired that it had been merely an exploratory landing and that many Canadians had been killed for apparently very little reward.

We often saw RAF and Polish squadrons of Spitfires and Hurricanes flying over the area as there was an airfield nearby at Woodvale. Although there was quite a strong air cadet corps at school, I deliberately avoided joining, preferring instead organisations and civil defence activity that didn't have the military ethos of flag-waving for king, country and the British Empire.

This is not a history of the war. Its annals have been well documented elsewhere. Like everyone else I had my own experiences and attitudes and was well aware that an optimistic gloss was being put on all news items for public consumption – and why not? A government must generate support and unify the nation in its common task of defeating fascism. There was also a simple logic that there must be a silver lining to every cloud and a sunny spell after every thunderstorm, so people had a right to expect happier times to come. On the other hand, if this kind of propaganda is overplayed, it can be counterproductive and cynicism develops, destroying people's moral fibre.

There were many stories of courage in the face of adversity and writers and film producers have always found them good sources to work on; on reflection though, I see that permeating society at the time was an ongoing discussion of what a post-war Britain would be like. Images of this were projected through documentaries in the cinemas on proposals for a national health service, education, New Towns and full employment, before the showing of the full-length films such as *Typhoon, How*

Green Was My Valley, *The Magic Bullet* or the Sherlock Holmes series and others that I remember seeing with my school friend, Ted Willis. Incidentally, he became a bank manager in Southport, but I was not to see him again; with much regret, my attempt to contact him was met with the news that he had just died of a heart attack.

Compared to pre-war, there was an increasing sense of community and friendship, of mutual help and sharing. There must have been crime but it was not much in evidence and I cannot remember any vandalism. Neither do I remember the back door of the house being locked, but some people had padlocks on their bikes and removed the lamp when leaving it.

Thus, the norms of human behaviour were established in my mind during my schooldays but in a wartime situation there is another ingredient. The resilience of the population is enormously helped by an external value system that goes beyond the welfare of the individual. Community values are enriched and the mental health and the quality of life of all are enhanced. I naively thought that these social attitudes would develop further into a socialist framework of society – 'from each according to his work; to each according to his need'. What went wrong?

Top: Sadie, Aberdeen, 1982.
Bottom: My extended family on the occasion of Aunt Marge's ninetieth birthday, Darwen, 1987.

Top: On the march, Aberdeen, 1964.
Middle: Aberdeen vigil, 1967.
Bottom: International anti-nuclear conference with Gordon
McLennan, Gen. Sec.CPGB, Berlin, 1982.

Top: Demonstration lesson for students, Aberdeen College of Education, 1964.
Bottom: Geography fieldwork, Gordale Scar, Easter, 1968.

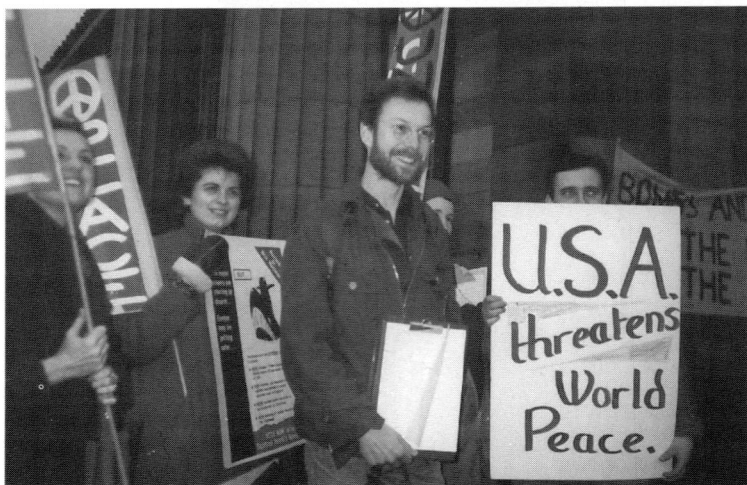

Top: May Day demonstration, Aberdeen, 1967.
Bottom: Demonstration by Stockbridge CND against American
bombing of Libya, Edinburgh.

Chapter IV
The Forties at Sea

> In the world through which I travel, I am
> endlessly creating myself.
>
> Franz Fanon

In my mid-teens I was consciously expanding my horizons
for greater opportunities and the gathering of fresh
experiences. I was studious to a point but loved the open
air.   In August 1943, together with my brothers and a
school friend, I cycled to the Lake District, slept in barns,
cooked on a methylated-spirit stove and sketched as we
rested. The others were 'real' artists and painted ready for
framing. I've rescued only a few of mine such as 'Grand
Nook, Hawkshead'.

For some, leaving home even for short periods and engaging in open-ended situations becomes stressful, and for a few even traumatic. I found such periods interesting and exciting and had no doubt that I would manage. I thought of those who couldn't cope as being rather abnormal. Of course there were certain apprehensions, but these were accompanied by the pleasure inherent in achievement. Such achievements did not need to be of the Everest-climbing variety, and indeed they were usually quite ordinary.

During several summer holidays I spent my time pea-picking on Booth's Farm, a few miles away. It supplied Hartley's Canning Factory at Aintree. Each person was given a row of peas to pick and the whole plant was stripped of its pods. The full basket was then weighed and a token received. Each forty-two pounds was worth 1s 3d. It matters little what the equivalent is in today's money, but it would have bought half a pound of bacon or three visits to the cinema.

Beginners could fill two or even three baskets in an eight-hour day, but skills could be improved and I regularly topped four. The banter and general rivalry, along with a need to earn more, led to challenges to pick a record amount. In the following summer of holiday picking I was filling six baskets a day, and on one occasion I worked overtime and reached a dizzy nine and was able to contribute to the family income accordingly.

In July 1943 I took the Joint Matriculation Board Exam with four A's (Distinctions) and four B's (Credits) and went into the sixth form. This was a two-year course for 'A' level in physics, chemistry and biology. As there was no biology taught at the boys' school, those opting for it went to the girls' high school on three afternoons a week. My declared ambition was to go to university and into agricultural research, but after two months in the sixth form I left school, to the astonishment and concern of the teachers. I loved the relaxed atmosphere of a sixth-form common room and the privileges that went with it such as not needing to wear a school cap! My chosen subjects were of great interest to me, but I didn't want to be called up into the services, resulting in a few years without getting any qualifications, as had happened to my father in the First World War to his later disadvantage. I was never persuaded to join the cadet corps but the open air seduced me into thinking of a career at sea until the war was over.

My friend, Teddy Woodall, had an uncle who had been a first mate in Elder Dempster Lines out of Liverpool, but having been torpedoed and traumatised by the experience he took a job ashore. I met him and saw his photographs. After a brief chat it confirmed my intentions. I handed in a note from my mother to the head teacher, and for the first time in my school career had a long talk with him in his study. My father contacted Elder Dempsters and I was given an interview in a large forbidding building next to that of the Royal Liver facing the Mersey. I also had to take the ferry to the other side at Birkenhead to be vetted by Blue Funnel Lines, the holding company following Elder Dempsters going into liquidation after an embezzlement of its funds before the war.

With Dad on my seventeenth birthday.

I was accepted as an apprentice deck officer, conditional upon successfully passing through an Outward Bound course at Aberdovey in Wales. The first vacancy was January 1944, so in the meantime I took a job on a farm and, a month later, as general dogsbody on a building site where they were putting up brick and concrete flat-topped houses for agricultural workers. I made the tea, stacked bricks, moved scaffolding and tidied up the site. The 'brickies' were exempt from 'call-up'. The labourers were middle-aged and rather indifferent to the work. The foreman was near to retiring and his main aim was satisfying the clerk of works with the least effort possible.

I began to understand the internal politics and contradictions of the workplace. It seemed to me that each was trying to hoodwink the other about what they were doing, often exaggerating the difficulties of the tasks in order then to be praised for doing it reasonably well. I noticed how the 'brickies' would converse in a different register depending on whether they were talking to their labourers, the foreman or the clerk of works. I earned their respect, not only by doing each job conscientiously, but because they knew I was waiting to go to sea where thirty-five thousand men had lost their lives, proportionately more than in the armed forces.

As long as the job was on schedule the contractor was happy, because he got his ten per cent on top of what it cost. If it rained the workers played cards in the hut, sitting on boxes and bags of cement. The toilet was a hut over a hole in the ground. A brazier was burning most of the time, using coke but started with wood from broken-up scaffolding – though timber was scarce, hence the flat concrete roofs. I often reflected on the fact that a central wall between two of the semis was wrongly placed, but it was too late to rectify the mistake and the clerk of works didn't measure it. What if the occupants discovered that their rooms were of a different size to those of their neighbours? I smile every time I imagine the subsequent scenes.

At lunchtime on Saturdays the foreman handed each worker his pay packet on which was written the number of hours worked and the amount enclosed. Workers at that time seemed to hand over their pay packets to their wives and were given their spending money in return. I followed the usual tradition with my mother. 'Can't fool the wife with this system,' says one. 'Oh yes we can,' says another, 'just put the money in your pocket and throw away the packet.' 'What?' says the first, 'tell the wife they've changed the system again?' – and so the conversation continued.

Overtime was usually genuine although sometimes inflated when the foreman saw that the job was getting ahead of schedule; but there was no pilfering or real criminality, unlike in the story related by one of the labourers. He'd just come from building runways at Woodvale for the Polish Spitfire squadron there. He described how surplus cement was sold off by reducing the specification and everybody bought off with a bit more overtime in his pay packet. I supposed that it would be some time before the runways crumbled.

Anyway, for most people it was a matter of survival and life had taught them to take opportunities where they existed. Take one day at a time and look after number one. Yet there was a common aspiration and a common good which also entered into the equation.

People were generally responsive to appeals to their better nature. For some it may have been lip-service, telling their friends in the pub of their good intentions.

The road to hell may have been paved by them, but only a cynic would have bragged about the uselessness of doing anything for anybody. In other words, there was a common assumption that 'I am my brother's keeper' – or perhaps it was just a tradition of working-class solidarity to counter the ongoing insecurity.

The word 'teenager' was not yet a part of everyday vocabulary. The aim was to grow up, hence the smoking behind the bicycle sheds which I had rejected after my first Woodbine – I have never smoked since, even though my parents did. At that time nobody connected smoking with any diseases and 'passive' smoking was not a phrase that existed.

So I felt that I was now entering the adult world, to start on life's adventure as a real person, no longer as a child. I was only sixteen, yet I now felt as though I could take on anything the world was going to throw at me – a necessary but illusory vision of youth.

★

In January 1944 I found myself at Aberdovey in Central Wales for what Kurt Hahn of Gordonstoun called training *through* the sea rather than *for* the sea. This was the fifteenth Outward Bound training course of four weeks of intensive physical and mental activity. From an early morning run and cold shower to evening talks on travel and navigation, from team work in boats to orienteering in the hills, from individually measured athletic achievements to seamanship skills, from cleaning the dormitories to Sunday church parades, the boys were testing themselves rather than being tested against each other.

I proved to myself that I could respond to any of the challenges put before me and this added to my self-confidence, but I also found that I had the confidence of others when I was given the task of leading a group on a three-day cross-country hike – these others including Clement Atlee's son and five other 'worthies'. I made all the various rendezvous as planned, and after a hot meal and a shower when we returned I felt as fit as a fiddle while the others were sleeping it off in their bunks.

The course was overtly aimed at character training, but it seemed that one had to have some character to start with or, like the few who couldn't give up smoking or be punctual, one would end up dropping out or going home. Some boys were surprised that there was no corporal punishment. It was habitually practised in public schools and in some sail-training establishments, but never in the Outward Bound schools.

On the occasions when I have volunteered to be one of a team or a committee I have never found such a role difficult to accept, even when decisions were made which I didn't agree with; but some people are unable to accept that position. Some think that because discipline is associated with a militarised structure there must be something wrong with it in civilian life. The key, surely, is whether the group cultivates an affiliative, supportive and caring attitude for all those within the group and teaches self-discipline?

There were some who didn't like the discipline but this was imposed more by the needs of the activities undertaken than by those supervising them. The sea is a good disciplinarian in this respect. We get so used to the idea that we are conquering nature, that we are in complete control as we turn on the taps, press the buttons, drive where we want to and eat when we like, that human behaviour is in danger of leading the world into an ecological catastrophe. At sea, teamwork is the norm. One's safety is dependent on the safety of all and co-operation is the name of the game. Outward-bound training is for life and is aptly named.

When I returned home it was time for me to get my kit together and prepare for sea. I signed my indentures as an apprentice deck officer, or midshipman as it was formerly known, on my seventeenth birthday, and joined my first ship, the *SS Calumet* in Hull. It was a typical cargo ship of the time, eight thousand tons gross, built at John Brown's on the Clyde in 1927, the year that I was born. Unlike the majority of ships it was steam-turbined with firemen and stewards from West Africa. Altogether there were fifty-six crew, but eight of these were naval gunners for the twin marlin machine guns, the Oerliken anti-aircraft and the four-inch howitzer on the stern. There were no guns on the foredeck as that would have classified the ship as offensive instead of defensive and different rules of engagement would have applied.

After a gunnery course at the end of the sand-spit of Holderness, the ship left in convoy heading north to Methil in Fife to take on coal for its own bunkers and also as cargo for Freetown. Routes and destinations were the subject of speculation and rumour as such information was known only to the captain. Neither was there any information about what was happening when the convoy was attacked. Apparently, German E-boats were approaching from the east and the escort ships saw them off in a blaze of fire power, but I had seen a better display of fireworks in the Liverpool blitz. When action stations were called it was a matter of picking up a duffel coat, tin hat and lifejacket and waiting. My job was to feed the ammo into the twin marlins as the DEMS gunner was firing, but fortunately they were never fired in anger during that voyage, only at practice drogues and logged accordingly.

Unlike some of my fellow crew members, I always made a safe passage and remained untouched throughout the war. No film simulates the long period of silence on watch, only the periods of depth-charging by the escorting frigates or planes and listening with relief as soon as the noise started to recede. It was a time to think, a time to look at the ever-changing sky, a time to watch the waves and the ship's wake, a time to reflect on what might be happening elsewhere and a time to wonder about the future.

Sometimes I tried to recall the words of a poem or song as I paced the bridge, swinging my eyes round the horizon. We had to keep a constant lookout and I discovered the technique for night vision. Specks of light are first detected at the sides of one's eyes. The binoculars can then be focused on them when the stronger signal can be seen by centring on them. I became quite good at recognising the stars, unpolluted by other light, and I pondered at man's insignificance in time and space. Then the officer of the watch would ask me to call the relief helmsman or make the tea.

Later I would have many more tasks to perform, including writing up the log, but now *Calumet* had rounded Cape Wrath and was anchored in Oban Bay on the west coast of Scotland, awaiting the arrival of ships for the next leg of the convoy.

The weather was good and the chief mate ordered lifeboat practice and rowing. That done, the crew mounted the rope ladders and winched the boats up on the davits. Myself and an African fireman were left to coil the ropes on our boat as it was hauled up out of the water, but one end gave way as the clutch on the winch disengaged. The fireman was thrown into the water, which was very cold at that time of year. However, my lifesaving training, my knowledge of what to do and my ability to respond meant that, for me, the reaction was as spontaneous as it was instantaneous. Without hesitation I jumped into the sea and rescued the fireman who was in a state of shock. My clothes were sent down to the boiler room to dry, a tot of rum arrived and that was the end of the matter. No big deal, of course, or so I thought; little did I know until I arrived back home five months later that it had been splashed over the front page of the local paper. The report, as usual, was suitably embroidered to make out that it was a courageous act by a young boy, when the reality was that it was almost run-of-the-mill in my thinking and it would be difficult to imagine anyone in a similar position not doing the same. The outcome was that I faced embarrassing moments when people commented on it later.

In retrospect, I maintained quite a common-sense, balanced view of the dangers at sea. I knew, for instance, that oil tankers carrying thousands of tons of highly flammable liquid were always in grave danger so they were placed inside the convoy. So too was it hazardous to be in the bowels of the ship in the engine room, whereas on deck all the safety equipment was at hand. I had no doubt about my surviving. All young men 'know' they are immortal, but I also knew that many merchant seamen had been traumatised by their experiences and could never sail again. Two of the training officers at the Outward Bound school were in that category. According to the wisdom of the mess deck it was impossible to predict who would be vulnerable to such stress – except that I felt I wasn't in that category. Thankfully, I was never put to the ultimate test.

At that time, the way to a skilled job was by means of an apprenticeship. There was a written contract or indentures and both parties had rights and obligations. There was little remuneration for the apprentice but the employer had responsibilities for his training and welfare. Normally the outcome of learning on the job was a career for life. In order that an appreciation of the totality of the profession was absorbed, the apprentice was given a taste of every conceivable task in the book, and most apprentices thought they were being used as cheap labour.

I never grumbled about the jobs I was given. It seemed to me that it was always a fresh experience and temporary at that, unlike those who had only that menial task to look forward to for the rest of their lives. Chipping rust and painting bilges were the worst; checking lifeboat stores in warm sunshine was the best. For example, the chocolate deteriorated and went white in the tropical heat and had to be replaced by new supplies, but it was not thrown away like the outdated pemmican, a high protein food packed specially for lifeboats.

Apprentices have always been the butt of practical jokes. One day I was sent to the bosun for a sky hook from the fog locker. The bosun, recognising that no such thing or place existed, kept his face straight and sent me to the second engineer who was working underneath the reserve generator down in the bowels of the ship. He reacted in exactly the same way and sent me to Sparks, the electrician, and finally to the skipper. At that point the penny dropped. I ended my wild goose chase by deliberately passing the bosun again, who by this time was engaged in serious conversation with Chippy the carpenter; I swore at him, to the amusement of everybody around. After that I was more alert and less naive, but also began to take jokes for what they were.

The deck apprentices were called cadets on this boat, although 'snotties' was used as the derogatory term, on account of the buttons on the cuffs of the uniforms designed to stop them wiping their noses with the sleeves!

We were given a correspondence course to follow. This included seamanship, rule of the road, signalling, naval architecture and cargo-handling, but by far the most important was navigation using *Nicholls Concise Guide* and *Nories Tables* of astronomical data. The exercises were posted at convenient ports of calls and were returned to the home address, so there was no immediate feedback.

Nevertheless, I kept to the suggested timetable and found it challenging but not difficult, and was pleased to be able to build on the maths and science I had successfully learnt at school. There were four cadets on the *Calumet* and two on subsequent boats. I found myself helping them, especially the ex-public school colleagues, who seemed to know a lot but understand little. It was actually very helpful to me, as teaching was a very effective way of reinforcing my own learning. Later there was a rumour spread by the skipper that I had won a sextant as first prize from the correspondence college. I was actually second and so ran to the same form as in my school days.

*

'All work and no play makes Jack a dull boy', a trite but true saying. My favourite pastime after reading and playing 'crib' – the best card game in the world for two people – was the music from the wind-up gramophone. The needle had to be changed after the flip side of the 78 record had been played, so there was always a big box of them to hand. When not in use the box of needles was put on the turntable, together with a tin of condensed milk and biscuits that were obtained from 'friends' in the galley, and the gramophone lid was closed. On one occasion, the ship was being thrown about by a force ten gale like a cork in a mountain torrent and we returned to find the gramophone on its side with the needles, condensed milk and biscuits not only scattered but all mixed up in a horrid-looking mess. As no more needles could be bought until reaching the home port these were very valuable, and so the evening was spent cleaning each one in turn. There was no reading nor crib nor Geraldo and Strauss that night.

A sketch I made showing some of the guns.
Photographs were not allowed.

At eleven each morning the captain went on his inspection round. To find fault he ran his finger along the top edge of the door and showed the dirt that had collected there. He inferred that the whole place was a pigsty even though we thought we had been meticulous in our cleaning. It didn't take long for us to substitute a radical clean-up with a wet rag wiped along the top of the door and a quick dumping of oddments in a bag that was temporarily hidden away. I stored an encyclopaedia of tricks of the trade so that when I became a skipper... but I never did.

The first experience of anything is etched permanently in the memory and then acts as a frame of reference which subsequent images amplify or modify. After a long trail out into the mid-Atlantic in convoy, going at the speed of the slowest, which was usually six knots, the *Calumet* arrived at Freetown in Sierra Leone, anchoring about a mile offshore. The panoramic view was straight out of the geography textbook, but ten times more detailed. What no photograph, film or description can convey are the smells, noise and general ambience of the scene. The air was humid and hot with sweat soaking and rotting each shirt on my back. A thought came to my teased mind. The olfactory nerve endings must be well-connected to the long-term memory areas of the brain, because the same smell or mixture of smells evokes the same visual scene and, by association, creates nostalgia.

The ship was surrounded by canoes with a colourful array of everything from bananas and fish to handmade baskets and carvings. Merely watching the bargaining of 'You come down and I go up' was fascinating, but to taste real ripe bananas was out of this world. Why is it that people all over the world like and dislike vastly different foods, but bananas and chocolate seem to be universally enjoyed?

Unloading a general cargo of crates and packages took a long time as each had to be checked. Care had to be taken lest those for the next port of call were dispatched in error, so straw matting was often used to separate one lot from the next. Not infrequently it happened that packages for one port of call were found at the next and I was given the job of checking, but at Takoradi on the Gold Coast a package was found destined for Freetown. I was hauled up before the first mate and given a dressing-down which I was always to remember. Cargo had to be checked and double-checked; containerisation has now simplified the system.

I not only tasted such exotic fruit as mangoes for the first time, but new items appeared on the menu like 'Palm-oil chop' accompanied by a variety of side dishes with ground nuts, peppers, coconut, 'garri' or boiled cassava, sweet potatoes and yams and a range of fruit. The crew were generally well fed as ship's rations were about double those of civilians, but access to other sources of food was very welcome.

On any ship, the quality of food depends on the chief steward and the cook. I had the highest regard for the work they put in, except when I noticed provisions going ashore instead of the other way round. I was only party to one such trade when the chief steward obtained crates of Cointreau, then unobtainable in Britain. My bottle was given to my mother who knew it was valuable and saved it for a special occasion. This never seemed to arise and years later, when it could be obtained from the corner shop, the same bottle was found in the cupboard.

After completely unloading the rest of the cargo in Nigeria, the *Calumet* proceeded south on her own as German U-boats had disappeared from the South Atlantic. We crossed the equator without any ceremony and sailed up the Congo to Matadi. The cargo that was taken on included ingots of copper from Katanga, mahogany and palm kernels. Beer in the Belgian Congo was cheap, strong and plentiful, and many of the sailors got drunk on it. There was also a welcome from the touts on the quay who offered to take anyone with spare cash for a good time with the girls. I tasted the beer, ignored the girls and took a long walk round the very attractive countryside dotted with magnificent villas not far away from areas of slums and shanties. I returned to the ship with a fever. It was malaria, probably contracted in Nigeria, and I was hospitalised in a Catholic institution. Because I had been taking the prescribed dose of quinine every day the Belgian nurses in nuns' habits injected me with massive doses; my temperature came down fairly quickly and I soon felt better. This was perhaps as well because the ship was due to sail.

It was now June 6th, 1944 and all the boats in the port were sounding off and being dressed with flags and bunting. The invasion of Normandy had at last begun and I reminded myself of the last three years of campaigning for the second front. Everyone realised that this was a turning point and the end of the war could now be envisaged, even though the Russians had been pushing back the Germans for some time. There was much less U-boat activity, but convoys were still necessary, except for the very fast ships like the *Queen Mary*.

The ship's purser put out daily bulletins on the notice board by the bar compiled from news that the radio operator had received. There were no other radios nor access to information, apart from the infrequent air letters from home which were picked up at Lagos and Freetown and were, naturally enough, about family and friends rather than the politics of the day. Sailing the world meant being isolated from it, a curious contradiction. The crew was a disempowered community on a desert island, floating around without means of communication with the outside world. This didn't seem to bother anyone except me. Was everybody out of step except me? Changing ships meant changing crews, with new gossip and new personalities, so I had many acquaintances, but few contactable friends. This seems to have been typical of sailors in general.

Most young men kept in contact with their families and girlfriends, but not their school mates, who seemed to disperse and get forgotten about. This was especially true of sailors, whose unpredictable leave onshore meant that it was difficult to pick up old friendships where they had been left off. Friends work, move, change their lifestyle and acquaintances, as well as finding new haunts without telling anyone.

I looked forward to the end of each voyage, especially when we anticipated a British landfall and the watches were doubled up. There was a certain satisfaction of a job well done, packing the gifts and being welcomed back, but it wasn't long before I looked forward to signing on for another voyage, a new crew and different locations. When I had said all my goodbyes and left the house with my kitbag and suitcase, I never turned back to give the last wave of farewell, or so I was told. My eyes looked expectantly ahead to new beginnings. My mind was always on the future and, again according to others, this was always the case. I enjoyed the present, but didn't live for it.

The next five trips were on the *David Livingstone*, a smaller diesel-engined cargo ship capable of carrying twelve passengers plus a doctor. On one occasion we left the convoy as it passed the latitude of the Canary Islands during the night and went into Tenerife at the port of Santa Cruz with a cargo of seed potatoes. The people looked desperately poor, many of them barefoot and in rags. I got talking to an English-speaking tally clerk who told me that two German U-boats had left the night before. Spain was supposed to be neutral but was an ally of the Nazis, and the Canaries were isolated and its people starving.

The British consul took myself and the other apprentice to the beautiful valley of Oratava, full of bananas on irrigated terraces stretching way up the hillside and flanked in the distance by the eleven thousand foot, snowcapped Mount Teide. On the quayside were hawkers of unsaleable goods, except for Swiss watches which were in very short supply in Britain, so I did a bit bartering for a couple of them. The *David Livingstone* joined another convoy to West Africa, and I supposed that the submarines were then allowed back to take on water and supplies after the gentlemen's agreement to let the British cargo of potatoes in first. There were still a few U-boats along the coast of Africa until the beginning of 1945, but then they disappeared and the ships went at their own speed.

In London's Albert Dock, however, it was much more dangerous, as the V1s and V2s came over without warning. Just as I was leaving the ship one evening there was a loud explosion not far away, followed by a whine. The rocket had struck before the sound of it reached the ears. There was no point in taking cover and everybody carried on as usual as the next one could be anywhere or nowhere. I went on to meet my sister Sybil, who was teaching in an Essex secondary school. Sitting in the 'gods' at the Sadlers Wells in Islington she explained how her class had been dwindling as the children described how so-and-so's house had been bombed or that another classmate had gone back to her aunt's in the country.

At home, there was a general acceptance of shortages, but I didn't see any real deprivation. It was now obvious that the allies were winning the war and morale was high with talk focused on 'after the duration'. There were Ministry of Information films and pamphlets, press features and talks on the radio about reconstruction. The Beveridge Report built up people's hopes and expectations of the prospect of a welfare state from the cradle to the grave, of new housing in neighbourhood units with libraries, nursery schools and community centres with youth clubs. There was going to be such a lot of work to be done that unemployment would be a thing of the past.

Like millions of others, I contrasted this picture of the future with that of the poverty, unemployment and hopelessness of pre-war times. Thus there was a feeling of optimism in adversity, a sense of purpose in society at large, a feeling that people would matter, have an equal opportunity and that the struggles would be worthwhile. I remember reflecting, 'Does man have to have an enemy to get the best as well as the worst out of him?' In contrast to the end of the First World War there was no mood at all for monuments, only reconstruction of both buildings and people's lives.

The Russians had conquered Berlin with terrible loss of life on both sides. The Americans met them as they advanced across the Rhine. The concentration camps were filmed and shown to cinema audiences, with names like Belsen and Auschwitz and a dozen others becoming symbols of man's inhumanity to man. Victory in Europe Day, VE day, was declared on May 8th, 1945; the *David Livingstone* was anchored off the village of Abonema in the Niger Delta, loading mahogany logs. The crew were given the day off and the motorised lifeboat was lowered as a ferry to the shore. There was nothing to do except to visit the market stalls, so I had a canoe paddle carved as a souvenir of the occasion that I had been so anxiously waiting for but not really believing in. Back on board I had time to draw a sketch of the panorama and have a couple of beers at the ship's bar before going to my bunk. The six years of war had seemed an eternity. It was, of course, one third of my life up to then, something we fail to register when we recollect how time is relative to our age. For example, at the age of sixty this period of the war would have been only a tenth of my life, and as anyone of that age will tell you, a previous year seems like a mere breath.

The war in the Pacific would continue for another three months, but everyone knew it was drawing to a close. One morning at breakfast in the saloon the message came through that an atomic bomb had been dropped on Hiroshima and had wiped it out. Initially there were cheers, but the conversation got round to the doubts about rivalries after the war. Did this end the war in the Pacific or was it the opening shot of a third round of hostilities?

I thought that the older men in the discussion were too cynical. We shall have a new international organisation, the United Nations, I said rather unconvincingly to those who remembered the old League of Nations. The next bomb on Nagasaki seemed to make even less sense as Japan was already suing for peace as the American battleships pounded the coast and Tokyo lay in ruins from massive bombing raids. Perhaps the new US President, Harry Truman, wanted to make sure the world knew his power, having half the world's resources and industrial production within his grasp.

Each one of the crew had a demob number, as did everyone in the armed forces. Unlike the end of the First

World War when the floodgates were opened by demobilisation and chaos resulted, those on active service would be allowed to leave in stages. This disappointed some who thought that the plum jobs would go to the first waves, but I had a career to follow. My apprenticeship was scheduled for four years, but due to a shortage of deck officers I was allowed to take the second mate's exam after three years at sea, so this was my immediate objective. My aim all along was to get qualifications and be in a position to choose my company or even seek and alternative career if necessary. At the back of my mind I was to have the security of a career and the prospects that my father never had.

Sailors get paid off at the end of the voyage minus any regular payments sent to the family and any 'subs' and bar bills spent at sea. At Liverpool the news came through that the 'danger money' would no longer be paid. This had been increased during the war instead of the basic so that take-home pay would plummet unless consolidated together. Now my remuneration, according to my indentures was nine pounds for the whole of the first year, twelve pounds for the second, fifteen pounds for the third and twenty-four pounds for the fourth, but the 'danger money' was one hundred and twenty pounds per year.

There was a spontaneous outcry when the 'danger money' was stopped, and I was slightly bemused when even the most conservative cadets declared they wouldn't go to sea until the marine officers' union got 'their money back'! How the ship-owners thought they could get away with it boggles the imagination. It was a complete throwback to their pre-war attitudes and practices. Needless to say the 'danger money' was then incorporated into the basic and the ships sailed again. They had to. The cargoes had to be shifted.

★

I collected my three war medals and they were not to see the light of day until forty years later at a demo of ex-services CND. My next trip was a short one across to Antwerp when the battleship *Missouri* carried Truman on his way to the Potsdam Conference. The two cadets were invited to go on a day trip to Brussels by an assistant in the British consulate. We dined in the Officers' Club at the tables occupied only a few months earlier by SS officers and were served by the same waiters, together with the same orchestra. I had never witnessed such a lifestyle. In contrast, the dockers were given huge spam sandwiches to maintain their energy to unload the ships. Seeing big American cars and luxury goods going into the warehouses I inquired about the destinations. The tally clerks recognised the consignees as Belgians who had made a lot of money in the Belgian Congo but had it frozen 'for the duration'. The products? Copper and Uranium, of course! The assistant consul was becoming very friendly and spoke of the mega-rich having kept their heads down or having even collaborated, but that now they were re-establishing themselves in the hierarchy of pre-war connections to continue exactly where they left off.

The host himself seemed to be full of contradictions as he fished for my views, but I was asking rather than answering. As the evening drew to a close, he invited my fellow cadet to stay the night with him or at least until later when he would take him back to the ship in a taxi. Everything became clear. He was a typical ex-public school homosexual. Why hadn't we recognised his intentions before? The two of us made a poor excuse that the skipper had expected us back already and we left. Come to think of it, my colleague had some of the same characteristics as this assistant consul: tall, flaxen-haired, gently spoken and with an elegant manner as he swung his hips and his hands.

On the way back to London the sea was calm with a beautiful mackerel sky. The general election results were coming over the radio: a landslide victory for Labour. There was elation all around. I was even surprised by the skipper's reaction. There was no doubt about Churchill's popularity as a war leader, but he had been the only card that the Conservative Party had been playing, whereas the issues had been jobs, education, the health service and above all, housing, and Labour had concentrated on a discussion of these. The electorate may have been apprehensive about the underlying difficulties and possible solutions, but they were ready to face the hard task of reconstruction.

Most elections are lost rather than won; that is, the incumbent government has failed to deliver and votes are cast against it rather than for an alternative. I believe that the 1945 election was different inasmuch as there was an all-pervading moral and cultural change demanding positive action. There was a flood of progressive ideas that would relegate conservatism to the dustbin of history, to be replaced by socialist policies.

However, the Communist Party proclaimed that the Labour Party had no overall strategy and principle so that it would give way under the pressures mounted by the defenders of the financial and industrial establishment. This was soon shown to be the case and even the newly nationalised industries of coal, gas, steel and the railways had boards appointed that saw their function to be that of underpinning and enriching the private sector. Foreign policy, especially under Bevin, became one of complete subservience to the United States.

Willie Thomson, the Glasgow historian and writer, has a similar view of those post-war years:

> ...wealth distribution remained unaltered, but more importantly tied the country to the US Military chariot, and the British economy to the requirements of the City and the Treasury, while continuing to play at being a great power. The consequences of these choices set the agenda for the next fifty years, profoundly infected the cultural climate and ensured that the economic and political crisis of the Seventies was resolved in favour of the right and not the left. Labour, when it has been in office since 1945, has, no doubt, tried its best to govern in the interests of the country at large. It had been forced into crises on each occasion and ultimately out of office because the City had been unwilling to tolerate even the mild degree of intervention that these administrations tried to sustain. The Labour governments were left beleaguered and vulnerable to the electoral bloc which could be mobilised against them.

> *New Times*, 1996

I quote this because it succinctly echoes my view. So, the economic situation got worse rather than better. British assets had been sold to the United States in order to buy weapons and food and the Empire's coffers were empty. The suppliers wanted hard currency and that meant dollars. Labour ministers went cap in hand to the financiers who imposed conditions that made them subservient to their demands for belts to be tightened and social reform to be halted. Rationing was more widely applied. The mines and railways had deteriorated through lack of investment before the war and overuse during it. Industry continued with the same tooling and concentrated on the short-term promotion of exports, with only limited utility furniture and clothes available for the home market.

The NHS was born and there was a lot of idealism in the air, but the wartime alliance of the USSR and ourselves was broken up, culminating in Churchill's Fulton speech. The cold war started, defence expenditure soared and not even the House of Commons was informed of the plans to build nuclear weapons. The hot war of British intervention in Greece, Malaya and India continued and Britain reverted to its role as an imperialist nation with a large contingent of forces in the five continents. It may have been a fiction during the war, but those who had wealth didn't seem to flaunt it. Now they did, but said they had no incentive to invest in British industry, so the Labour Government felt that they were in a catch-22 situation. Whose interest were they going to serve? Incentives had to be given to the financiers, but not to the working population, and strikes resulted.

During the war the Communist Party, of which my parents were members, gave priority to the strengthening of the trades unions and this paid dividends to working people after the war and many historians like Nina Fishman, now recognise this. We heard over the radio about the dockers and how they were holding the country to ransom, but

90

nothing about the 'strike' of capital in failing to invest in socially desirable projects at home, so some (the rich) were given carrots and others (wage earners) were given the stick. The electorate were becoming increasingly disillusioned and the Tory Housewives League went on the offensive with full press support, yet the Labour Party couldn't even produce a daily paper to present their interpretation of events and so backtracked on their promises.

★

My next ship was the SS *Cochrane*, the sister ship to my first, the *Calumet*, and sailed for a whole year between West Africa and the United States. I became competent in Great Circle sailing and identifying with pinpoint accuracy the crossing of the Gulf Stream off Cape Hatteras by the simple means of measuring the sea temperature. I called in at such ports as Philadelphia and Baltimore, but the longest stays were in New York, moored alongside the old wooden jetties on the Brooklyn side. During the day I assisted with the unloading of cocoa and hardwoods and the loading of general cargo – from cars to packets of shoes. I was usually a couple of weeks in port which gave ample time to take the subway, or 'underground', into the centre of Manhattan.

The shops were full of consumer goods of all kinds, having been produced continuously throughout the war. When questioned, some Americans complained that they had to wait for their orders for a new car to come through, as though it were a terrible hardship. It is true that in the American press at the time there were reports of young couples having to sleep in their cars because they couldn't get a house, which rather amused me, knowing that all car production had stopped in Britain and that the pre-war tooling had then been brought out of storage to produce cars after the war like the old Ford Anglia and Prefect.

To prevent profiteering the American Administration had controlled prices, but when I handed over the exact money for a bar of chocolate I was told to hand over another twenty-five per cent with the comment, 'If you don't want it you needn't have it', so it boiled down to market forces – if you had the money you could get anything.

At the cadet club in 42nd Street, not far from the Rockerfeller Centre, stood a coke machine and a jukebox. On Tuesday, Thursday and Saturday nights girls were chaperoned to and from the club with a dancing teacher. The lessons were followed by a few of the records, the cadets taking turns to put in a nickel for their choice. The quickstep was my favourite and remained so until I learnt the tango after I had retired! There was also a blank record for five minutes of peace and quiet, especially when someone wanted to have a conversation with their partner. I wrote to one of the girls when I knew of my approximate date of arrival on the next trip, only to discover that she had moved meantime to Minneapolis, at that time three days away from New York by train.

No one else appeared on the scene in which there was mutual attraction until a passenger boarded at New York bound for Lagos. Miriam was a girl just out of college, going to a mission school in Onitsha on the Niger. When I was off duty we used to meet at the stern, leaning over the rail, listening and looking at the wash from the propeller, discussing what our ideals were: an ideal home, an ideal garden, an ideal holiday, right through to an ideal world. As William McIlvaney observed in *The Kiln*, 'Ideals were like items you packed in your luggage and took with you everywhere and then never got to wear.' By this time I was searching for a relationship, but not knowing much about it. Strange to say I had no problem controlling the sexual component, whereas years earlier it was a question of going to bed with a sexual problem on my mind and waking up with the solution on my belly!

*

I succeeded in getting three days' leave in Lagos and flew via Benin in an old De Havilland Dove over the extensive rainforest, crossed by the occasional red laterite road. Miriam took me round a leper colony and a palm oil plantation, as well as the school where a class was learning the Tudor period of English history for the London external exams. Most of the pupils seemed to have ambitions to be doctors, lawyers or accountants. None were interested in agriculture, transport or the social services, which I naively thought would equate more appropriately with the country's need.

Miriam was carefully chaperoned by the headmistress, and I stayed at the house of a male teacher, who with evangelical zeal, tried unsuccessfully to engage me in theological debate. I was no medieval Jesuit who could argue how many angels could stand on the point of a pin. On the third day I returned to Lagos by road in the first class compartment, that is, the cab of a 'mammy' wagon, an ordinary truck with hard benches and luggage, chickens and children, in addition to a full complement of adults in their colourful Lancashire cottons.

I lost Miriam's address, but she eventually wrote from Canada to say that her friend was touring Scotland and that she had given her my address in the hope I could be of assistance, but it was a cold letter and I didn't reply, although I did see the friend. That was all.

★

In January 1947, I enrolled at the Liverpool Nautical College for a three month course for the Ministry of Transport's Second Mate's Certificate of Competency (Foreign Going). Britain was enduring one of the longest cold spells of the century and the power stations couldn't keep up with the demand, dropping the voltage or cutting out for hours at a time. After two months I took the exam and passed all eight parts at the one diet. I immediately went to the Ministry of Labour Inquiries Office for details of college courses and applied for a place on the Emergency Training Scheme for teachers of further education. The Butler Act envisaged a big expansion in all the sectors, and I had read about and taken a keen interest in the new county colleges that were going to be set up, with compulsory part-time day release for all young people until they were eighteen.

I went back to sea as third mate on the *MV Sangara* which I had seen beached in Lagos lagoon during the war with a big torpedo hole in its side. It had now been completely renovated. I now had a cabin of my own and I felt on top of the world, even though I was actually waiting for about two years for a place at college. I really enjoyed the responsibilities of navigation, cargo-handling on the foredeck and safety checking. I was especially good at loading logs of hardwood because they were all shapes and sizes and weighed up to six tons, so a whole variety of arrangements with wire ropes and blocks had to be used.

The dockers were skilled but would take the easy ways rather than the most efficient storage positions, so I reckoned I had to lead from the front to get the maximum tonnage in the hold. Another of my favourites was loading bulk groundnuts. Down below men had to shovel the nuts to the side, right up to the deckhead to fill the hold to its maximum extent, but they got tired and held up the loading through the main hatch by not shifting it fast enough. I went down and devised the scheme whereby one side worked like the devil as the flow of nuts poured in while the other side rested. Through the 'headman', to whom I had given a draught of rum, I explained the procedure; I blew a referee's whistle which was the signal for a change-over of the teams working.

They were warned that the nuts would keep flowing in. The result was that I not only loaded the maximum possible in the hold but finished before the others, that is, the gangs supervised by the first and second mates. But there was another factor. These African dockers started at six and finished at six; that is, all the hours of daylight. Instead of merely telling the headman to get on with the job in the morning and then going to breakfast, I stayed on deck for an hour and checked that there were no weak points, any one of which could hold up the rest of the loading, and then went for breakfast.

This 'leading from the front' became a characteristic of mine and was what I enjoyed most. I was known to have progressive views and in consequence I was chided as a slave driver. My reply was that the dockers should have a trades union to negotiate conditions rather than expect me to turn a blind eye if some were found asleep because they were tired, ill or ill-fed.

I then moved, as second mate to a coaster, *MV Oxford*, taking coal from Port Harcourt to the Gold Coast. Rather a quick promotion, I was now responsible for the medical chest as well as navigation. Against a numbered list of symptoms and ailments was a list of medicines and tablets, and I used to tell some of the crew that, for instance, I hadn't got a number nine tablet so I'd give them a four and a five. It was amazing that they still had confidence in me. On the other hand I had the key to the 'packets of three' (condoms), so they had to be nice to me. I also organised a social club which all the crew could join, playing bingo in the main saloon, which was really the preserve of the mates and engineers, but I convinced the skipper that it would be good for morale.

I got the money out of the company for a football strip and boots and we challenged other boats who played in their ordinary footwear. However, it soon became evident that no one was really capable of running about for so long and the skipper said their work was suffering. I felt it was not worth any hassle and agreed, especially as I now had a correspondence course in geography to follow. I thought that this course was expensive at the time, but as I had paid for it I made sure this Cambridge firm gave me value for money, regularly returning scripts to be marked.

★

In the equatorial region there is no weather, only climate. It's the same every day all the year round, 27°C, becoming overcast as the day wears on, ending with heavy thunderstorms and a pleasant enough evening. One day, the sky darkened and the hatches were closed in anticipation of a heavier than usual thunderstorm, but it seemed to me rather unusual. The birds went silent and the night life began to emerge. I dashed up to the chart-house and checked the nautical almanac. Sure enough, the track of a total eclipse of the sun passed over Port Harcourt at that very moment, so I bellowed from the bridge to uncover the hatches and restart the loading. I remember as though it were yesterday the faces of incredulity looking at me from all directions. I waved with the almanac in my hand, and said it was an eclipse and got them all working as daylight was re-emerging. By this time the skipper was on deck wondering why the activity on the foredeck was so different from aft. He gave me a knowing thumbs-up sign, and I hope it wasn't arrogant of me to feel a glint of self-satisfaction.

It may seem strange that my career should be elsewhere when I was so obviously good at my job, was generally liked although I didn't play to the gallery, and enjoyed the work immensely. Job satisfaction has always been the dream of anyone in employment, but all the older members of the crew, including the officers, were frustrated at rarely seeing their families, and even more rarely during the school holidays and at Christmas – more ships used to leave port on Christmas Eve than on any other day of the year because it cost the company money to allow them to stand idle. The second reason was my interest, not only in my work but in education and world affairs, and in having a social life.

It made me realise that if I stayed at sea too long it might jeopardise my chances of ever getting a job ashore, getting married, settling down and raising a family. My reading and reasoning reinforced my intentions. My demob number was now up and I just had to wait for the London College for the Training of Technical Teachers to confirm their provisional acceptance and provide a place in the General Subjects Department, or 'County College' group as it was then called.

After nearly six years at sea the salt water gets into your blood, or so everybody was telling me, so I decided to write down my thoughts on my expectations ashore. Unfortunately, I've lost those, half a dozen pages, mixed up no doubt with a lot of other useless baggage from the past and long since jettisoned. This is not without significance. I knew what I wanted to do, but others cautioned me with advice. I would love those papers to turn up: a) because I know I was unambiguous about the decisions I was making and how I felt at the time, and b) because I wonder what it was that gave others the impression that I may not have thought things through and that I may therefore live to regret redirecting my life into an entirely different course of action?

It also happened when I left school and it has punctuated my life since. The vibes I have transmitted have obviously contained confused signals, whereas I have viewed the major changes as merely evolutionary; hence the 'no turning back' syndrome has been due to a 'better things ahead' attitude... *Je ne regrette rien.*

Chapter V
The Fifties in England

He thinks too much. Such men are dangerous.

Julius Caesar, 1.2.196

In September 1949 I entered the London College. There were two newly established colleges to train teachers for further education; the other one was in Bolton. The London College was housed in the North-Western Polytechnic in Camden Town. Out of the hundred or so students, fifteen were in the county college group to teach mainly English and Social Studies to day-release students from fifteen to eighteen years of age, most of whom would be taking various technical courses. At twenty-two I was the youngest, but already I had six years of industrial experience, the entry qualification on this special Emergency Training Course. A two-year course was condensed into ten intensive months in order to produce as many teachers as possible for further education, as it was envisaged that day-release of one day per week would be made compulsory as proposed in the 1944 Education Act. There was not only a shortage of teachers but also of specialists in day-release.

A fellow student, Ruth Massie, invited me to a meeting of the Hampstead branch of the Communist Party at which her father, Professor Hyman Levy, was speaking, and after reading one of his books I joined the party, but took no active role then as I was concentrating on my studies and preparation for teaching practice. I lived in the hostel in Swiss Cottage from Monday to Friday. My parents and sister had moved to a house in Perivale, Middlesex. I went there on most weekends and with them joined the operatic society to sing in Gilbert and Sullivan's *Pirates of Penzance*, and in following years, *Gondoliers* and *Mikado* in which I sang the title role.

At the Christmas dance in the Women's Hostel I got into the swing of things, especially with the quickstep and waltz that I had learnt at the cadet club in New York. I found myself relating more and more to Mary, a dressmaking and tailoring student from Leeds. In the spring and summer terms we met more frequently, at the cinema or on Primrose Hill. Finally we became engaged to be married sometime the following year when we had got our jobs and plans for the future rather more settled than was the case on leaving college. As everybody appreciated, it was normal then to have a long-term view of marriage preceded by a long engagement and, of course, no premarital sex.

Because it was a shortened course a successful outcome depended on further approved studies as well as probationary teaching. I enrolled for the Inter B.Sc. course, the equivalent of 'A' levels, at Kingston Technical College, housed in some leaky prefab buildings, but with some reasonably good teaching. I bought a new drop-handlebar bicycle as I had taken a job at Hydon Heath Camp School near Godalming in Surrey, some fifteen miles away, where pupils from Essex secondary schools went on a four-week course, combining studies in and out of the classroom. As compensation for the extra duties in the evenings and alternate weekends the staff were boarded free, so it was possible to save. There was also no time and money wasted travelling to work. This characterised the whole of the community a few decades ago, when people lived next to the factory, office, school or other place of work. Now it is difficult to find anyone who is not spending more time and money commuting.

The Korean War started in 1950 and the immediate effect at home was to send prices up. I bought some blankets as soon as I saw that the price of wool had shot up and it wasn't long before this was reflected in the shops. Seeing these blankets on our bed for the next twenty years never failed to remind me of the savings I had made. Of course, the Korean War was much more serious than that. Two million lives were lost and many more millions wrecked. The whole weight of the United States was now engaged in a 'hot war'. Stalin kept out of it. There was also increasing concern about the threats that were being made to drop nuclear weapons on the Chinese when they intervened and pushed the Americans back. What interested me at the time, and which has subsequently been vindicated as fact, is that Atlee, yearning for the alliance, made a dash across the Atlantic for an emergency meeting with the US President, to plead restraint on General MacArthur, who intended to drop nuclear weapons in order to defeat the Chinese. Later I was to hear Professor Ritchie-Calder give a 'blow-by-blow' account of the anguished Cabinet decision in the face of growing public concern, especially within the ranks of the Labour Party, although at the time suggestions to this effect were being denied.

Now that the archives of the Soviet Union have been opened up and are being studied, a fresh light is being shed on their handling of international affairs, and Paul Lashmar, a BBC producer, has reported that Stalin told Kim Il Sung that it was 'not advisable for North Korea to engage in offensive action against South Korea', despite the activities of the American-installed and 'aggressive nationalist leader, Sygman Rhee'. It is true that at the time, those of us on the left supported the Russian stance and opposed the American one on principle. Of course, the issues were not so black and white, but America had over one hundred and fifty bases encircling the Soviet Union and acted as the world's policeman. It was important to defend the Soviet position when the whole of the establishment and the media were engaged in an hysterical campaign against it. *Realpolitik* is not an easy concept to handle.

The archives of the United States are now being made available through their 'Freedom of Information Act', and a documentary on BBC2 in 1996, *Baiting the Bear*, told the story of General Curtis Le May's 'Project Control'. He was the Commander in charge of America's Strategic Air Command of nuclear bombers. Unknown to President Eisenhower, he had his finger on the nuclear button without the need for presidential clearance, and went ahead with overflying the Soviet Union, deliberately seeking a pretext for a nuclear attack. President Kennedy was horrified, but was told by Le May's deputy that he'd regard it as a victory if only one Russian and two Americans survived. Today we seem even luckier to be alive than we thought yesterday!

It may be true that many of us were naive about 'Russian National Interests' but my opinion now does not differ much from the views I held then. The Cold War was in full swing. The free-for-all in the global market place was dominated by the United States, but the Soviet bloc was closed to it. The drive for maximum profits was also limited by socialist ideology and action in Europe, and John Foster Dulles proclaimed that the role of the West was to 'roll back Communism' and defeat the advance of socialism, especially in Italy, France and Britain. The Labour Government had already declared its unquestioning loyalty to the White House, mainly for economic reasons, and had 'proved' itself with military action around the globe, as in Malaya, Greece, India, Kenya, Aden and other places 'in the national interest', a catch-all phrase when there's a hidden agenda in the interests of the wealthy few.

At that time the United States announced a huge increase in 'defence' expenditure. It initiated the founding of NATO, insisting that it would always be headed by an American general 'to protect our national interests', as Congress put it. The Soviet Union responded likewise and the Warsaw Pact was formed. The arms race had begun.

Those who had struggled against poverty and unemployment in the Thirties, had seen active service during the war and had suffered the privations after it, were now becoming disillusioned with the Government in which they had put their faith. I could see the dilemma of members of the Labour Party who wanted social progress but had to support a Labour Government which was increasing taxes to pay for rearmament, going back on its promises, which led to its defeat at the polls.

1951 was the year of the great Festival of Britain, one hundred years after the Great Exhibition of 1851 which had heralded Britain's overwhelming dominance of world industrial production and trade. Mary and I went to see it while in London as there was already some controversy about it. It was supposed to mark the end of post-war gloom and the press hyped it up as the greatest ever. Yes, it was worth seeing, especially the displays of science and technology. However, I was disappointed in the cultural and political aspects with the kaleidoscope of oddments – our royal heritage to national orchestras, bagpipes and cricket. There was no social history nor vision expressed about the British people. There was a complete exclusion of the labour and trades union movement, yet it was a Labour Government that had commissioned and paid for it. It was just as if it had been put into the hands of Conservative Central Office to organise, with their nostalgia of the Empire and England's 'green and pleasant land', with a lot of stale ideas thrown in about the future of consumer growth.

We were invited to Ruth's for a meal afterwards. She put her toddler to bed and her husband was late home, working on a research project involving cosmic rays from outer space. I kept in touch. Ruth remarried, but a few years later she died of bowel cancer so that I never managed to get to grips with the political and philosophical questions we had started to discuss in the Old Students' Association after leaving college.

I remember well that 1951 was also the year of the publication of the Communist Party's *British Road to Socialism*. It marked a departure from the 'Comintern' days in that it described an independent and parliamentary way for Britain, whether or not this was appropriate for other countries. The Soviet Union was recognised as the 'leading force' because its collapse would inevitably be a defeat for all, so that no dirty washing was washed in public and international solidarity was regarded as the key to any progress anywhere. However, it was not so much the global as the local that energised the political campaigns, but by this time I was fully engaged in the building of my own future. Mary and I were married in August 1951 in Leeds and honeymooned near Grantham. This was one month after my brother, John, had graduated as a doctor, and had emigrated to the States as an intern at a hospital in Trenton, New Jersey.

We bought a terraced house at 33 Sherwood Avenue, Greenford, Middlesex. We had put all our money down as a deposit on it, so it was only by gradual increments that we added one bit of furniture after another, starting with a bed and a Vono card table, and eventually buying an old second-hand fridge. We then reached the dizzy heights of being able to buy, from Hammersmith Co-op, a Goblin washing machine that had just come on to the market.

Our time was particularly taken up with preparation for school lessons but, in addition, I had enrolled for a four-year course at Birkbeck College of the University of London leading to an honours degree in geography. This meant travelling straight from work by tube to Central London every evening, and for fieldwork in geology and geography, on many weekends and during the holidays, with Mary often accompanying me, notably to Malham, Swanage, East Midlands and Salisbury. During the week I regularly made up my sandwiches the night before and the next morning took them out of the fridge to eat on the train after school on my way to college. On one occasion, I unwrapped them and saw just raw bacon! I had taken the wrong package out of the fridge, so I was forced to starve until I got home at ten that night.

Mary and I were both keen gardeners, growing an ever-widening range of flowers and vegetables, with new ventures every year such as mushrooms under the new greenhouse benches, dahlia and chrysanthemum propagation, tree-felling and some bricklaying, and entering the local horticultural shows with Mary getting the prizes for her crafts and baking. She was highly thought of by the neighbours, but I was too occupied with the university course to get to know anybody except to pass the time of day. As time went on, teaching became both easier and more rewarding, and I seemed to have surprised my colleagues in the staff room by describing how the job was more exciting and satisfying than sailing the oceans during the war! I further confounded them by my explanation of how much I liked the Merchant Navy, navigating, loading cargo and meeting people, but that the future of the British people lay in the increasing reservoir of skills and knowledge of the pupils.

I liked teaching, including the clichéd 'challenge' of trying to motivate pupils, whose aim, often enough seemed to be an attempt to resist learning. Was this just the idealistic ramblings of a misguided young man? After all, it was only a secondary modern school with no external exams. The pupils found work as soon as they left school. Expectations were low, with pupils, parents and teachers alike. It was a 'good' area compared to Central London, so that discipline was not a great problem, but there was a rapid turnover of teachers. Soon I gave the impression to pupils (now called students) that I had been built with the school and wedded to its routine.

Mary and I had deliberately delayed having children until we had established ourselves financially, with a home ready to receive demanding babies, but then none arrived. The stork had forgotten us. However, after what seemed an eternity of visits to the Royal Free Hospital in Central

London, our first-born, Pamela, arrived on May 15th, 1956 in Perivale Maternity Hospital, just before I was to take my final exams.

At that time, fathers were not allowed to be present at the birth, only entering the ward an hour later. All was well and mother and baby were sent home after a short few days, with no respite for either of them, twenty-four hours a day, seven days a week, and it was an act of great understanding and friendship that Mary and baby Pamela were invited to stay with the Cranes, a colleague's family, during the nine days of my exams. My only regret has always been that I had not compensated them for 'saving the day', enabling me to get a good honours degree and the passport to a lectureship in geography and social studies at Carshalton College of Further Education.

Before the war only four per cent of the population owned a car. In 1950 there were three million on the road. By 1980 this had risen to twenty million, and we are now locked into a car culture that is a threat instead of an asset. What do I remember of 1956? An increasing number of cars were being produced in Britain and imported cars were a novelty and expensive. There was a waiting list which varied according to the model; about eight months for a Morris Minor, my first choice, and five months for an Austin A30. There were models like the Ford Prefect, in which the driving school had taught me to pass the test, and there were pre-war designs when the machine tools were put to one side and resurrected afterwards.

Modified forms were then built like the 'new' Ford Anglia. My sister purchased one and used to take us all, including our parents, to the seaside at Worthing or Brighton. Austin had brought out a small van which was exactly the same as the saloon, except that there were no windows or seats in the back. However, the vans were much cheaper as they were not taxed, so I bought a new one for £360 and, with the help of colleagues, I put in the rear windows and Mary upholstered the back seats. Subsequently, this became common practice, until the government imposed the tax on such changes. Appending price tags is tempting because it becomes amusing, like filling the tank with petrol and getting change from a one pound note, but an idea of money equivalence can be gained from the fact that the A30 had cost about the same as the annual starting salary of a teacher, so we are talking in roughly the same terms today.

Over the summer holidays of '56, Mary and I went house-hunting with baby Pamela in the detachable top of a pram at the back of the car, and removed to a delightful three-bedroomed semi with garden and garage at the end of a cul-de-sac in Caterham-on-the-Hill. Pamela didn't seem to need much sleep and many were the times when she was taken for a ride in the car or pushed round the streets to get her off. We erected a greenhouse, cut down a giant Wellingtonia that seemed to be dying and was mentioned by neighbours as a possible threat in a gale. The end of my studies gave me more spare time, even though I took seriously the preparation for college including fieldwork at weekends and during the Easter holidays. However, I began to take up an interest in the college branch of the Association of Teachers in Technical Institutions (the ATTI), the local branch of the Communist Party and then the newly formed Campaign for Nuclear Disarmament (CND), taking groups to Aldermaston marches.

Teaching fifteen to eighteen year olds was the aim of my college training, so that I was now working in the milieu of my choice in a newly built college with excellent facilities and an enthusiastic staff. I loved it and couldn't avoid doing well. I took day-release classes for an hour's English and social studies and a full-time class for geography to 'O' level. These students had left secondary modern schools with no examination classes, as they were labelled by the system as 'non-academic', which is one reason for doing practical and fieldwork to make understanding and motivation primary objectives – and the exam results proved the efficacy of the method.

There was suddenly a new interest in higher education by the Establishment after years of resistance to any form of expansion. The space firsts by the Soviet Union had sent shock waves around the educational and political institutions of the West. The question was asked in the media and elsewhere – how could a nation, not long after it had been devastated by war and then isolated in peace, catch up, let alone overtake the USA which had, in contrast, come out of the war with an economy vastly expanded and technologically advanced.

Only one answer could be found and that was a massive investment in a broad-based educational system leading to a pinnacle of technological excellence. The political will in the West was lacking until then, but the response by the British, as with the American Government, was immediate and a crash programme of expansion in technical and higher education was under way. Apart from very welcome salary increases there were other effects. Before the contract for the college tennis courts was completed, plans were agreed for extending the building in their place. However, the contractors evidently had to be allowed to complete the tennis courts, so the day they were so beautifully finished the bulldozers came in and ripped them up.

In general the staff at the college were in their thirties and forties – at their optimum in terms of experience, knowledge and skill. They were a co-operative and kindly lot, despite some of the names – Messrs. Basham, Savage and Kille! Union membership was one hundred per cent and I eventually became branch secretary and then assistant secretary for the Surrey Division. Apart from the immediate problems we discussed long-term policies as indicated, for instance, in the Robbins Report.

I also remember discussing the drafts of resolutions for National Conference, especially the controversial ones on peace, disarmament and the redeployment of resources committed to 'defence' into education and health. Across the other side of the county I had long discussions with a like-minded Jack Tyrell, benefiting from his insights into the strategy and tactics of promoting policies and actions that the right wing were already anticipating and countering – and they had the press and money at their disposal. It wasn't a question of smoke-filled rooms and secret deliberations and instructions, but the Communist Party had 'aggregate' meetings of members which enabled the leadership to know what was happening at grassroots level and enabled individuals to benefit from the overall picture and to word resolutions appropriately to have the maximum chance of success.

The media, reflecting the policies of the establishment, continually referred to subversion and 'entryism' by 'alien' groups. This may have occurred with certain sectarian and ultra-left individuals, but my experience was the exact opposite. The Party devoted time, resources and energy that strengthened the union and the interests of its members with no direct benefit to itself. Indeed, my union work was escalating at the expense of the political and peace campaigning and later, when I moved to Scotland, I reversed these priorities.

Blacklisting by employers via the Primrose League and MI5 went unchecked and an outstanding fellow member of the Communist Party, Eric Atkinson, has detailed how he was unjustifiably dispossessed of his livelihood by such means. The actions of MI5 spies in CND and the CPGB have been exposed by whistle-blowers like Clive Ponting, and especially Kathleen Massiter who was imprisoned because she could no longer tolerate the misuse of the secret services to support the conservative policies of the Government. For example, in 1983 Thatcher gave Heseltine the task of campaigning against CND and exposing communist influence in it. Amusingly, it backfired when his spies reported that instead of communists influencing CND policy it was CND that was influencing Communist Party policy. Until the Nineties I was refused a visa by the United States but I had the satisfaction of embarrassing the officials of the then US Consulate in Edinburgh when I discussed it with them. It is interesting that now, in the Nineties, the Data Protection Registrar, Elizabeth France, has asked MI5 to ensure that its files on over one million British citizens are accurate, relevant and up to date but MI5 have refused to involve any Government watchdog, so who knows what happens behind the cloak of unnecessary secrecy? As Jimmy Reid has described (*Scotsman*, August 29th, 1997), 'Historically and currently, British security services have equated defence of the realm with defence of the political *status quo*. Those who challenged or wanted to change that *status quo* were considered subversives or traitors; often accused of being agents of a foreign power. The real traitors (such as Blunt, Burgess, McLean, Philby and Cairncross) were considered sacrosanct because they had the right public school accents and contacts... The national security of Britain was thereby nearly strangled to death by the old school tie.' In reality, therefore, the traitors were found on the playing fields of Eton and in the ivory towers of Oxbridge; never in the Communist Party of Great Britain.

Mary had no objection to me taking an evening class as that was more money coming in, but problems seemed to emerge as I attended to my outside interests. It was a dilemma that I forced myself to put to one side because I had seen so many who could have made an enormous contribution to one cause or another but seemed to be locked into a domestic prison. One would normally think of a compromise solution, but does one go to half a conference or half a demonstration or take on half the secretary's job which, being voluntary and with no other nominations, might result in the collapse of everything you want to happen? I therefore decided to live with conflicting loyalties, knowing that evil would triumph if we didn't 'have time to do anything about it'.

★

Everybody tries to rationalise what they do in order to justify their actions, but it seemed to me that the role of irrationalism in human affairs is not only exceedingly powerful but detrimental to the interests of others, and therefore, in the longer term, to oneself. If animals don't do the right thing they don't survive, so they tune in very sensitively to the real world around them.

Biologically humans are animals, but they are qualitatively different in their level of sophistication to the extent that they have the capacity to delude themselves as they struggle to match their emotional and intellectual responses. Why could this be?

Briefly, I would summarise it like this. The lower parts of the brain are programmed at birth, so that we can operate on automatic for much of the time. However, the higher parts involve a learning process, becoming actively engaged in making billions of interconnections in the construction of a very complex model of the world, as referred to in chapter one. This model acts as a frame of reference for subsequent input via the sense receptors leading to action or to its internalisation, which we call thinking and imagining. Humans do this consciously but this often comes into conflict with our baser instinctive feelings of fear, lust, envy, passion, greed, aggression and so on. How often, then, does our intellect accept something that our 'heart' doesn't, and vice versa?

The problem for me was how to accommodate this conflict of what I thought to be the necessary course of action propelled by long-term global considerations of changing society to work in the interests of the majority rather than a rich and powerful minority, as against my short-term interest in day-to-day family duties and pleasures.

It seemed to me at the time, as now, that these powerful élites perpetuated their positions by the exploitation of the irrational to the extent that religion, magic, superstition, legend, myths, cults and mystical philosophies have been used to retard human progress. On the other hand, these aspects of the human condition have always been with us and therefore must be part of a human need and even the most intelligent have been drawn to a belief in the supernatural. Having turned it over in my mind I concluded that, for instance, people need religion and other illusions as a solace in an unkind world, as an answer to the interminable questions that arise every day. It doesn't follow, however, that it's true. It may also be a fact that it makes law and order easier to maintain, just as Moses had to say to his unruly followers when he came down from the mountain with the commandments in tablets of stone that it was God who had given them to him. Life is much easier if we can invoke a higher authority, which makes the road to democracy so difficult to achieve, let alone the road to Socialism.

My experience seemed to suggest that those interested in furthering their own interests in politics with status, recognition, power, a career and future prospects had to pander to the lowest common denominator, be charming to their colleagues, the electorate and especially the media. They also had to engage in slinging as much mud as possible at the opposition and to devise enough gimmickry to gain attention. In contrast, long and detailed discussion and debate of policies were certainly the order of the day in the Communist Party because this was no ladder of opportunity for the careerist politician but only for those interested in a commitment to a struggle on behalf of the disadvantaged majority of the population.

As one of my esteemed colleagues in Aberdeen, Annie Inglis, was later to remark, with the appropriate amount of academic cynicism, I seemed to have got the knack of campaigning for lost causes! Actually, it was a case of 'win some lose some' but however many 'battles' we lost we were sure we would win the 'war'. We told each other that history was with us. We believed in 'progress' and the ability of man to decide his own future, but for this we had to study the jungle warfare of capitalism in order to change society to a more just, fair and peaceful one, and in changing the world for the better we changed ourselves for the better. As the Chinese would say, the longest journey starts with a few steps.

Thinking globally and long term starts with thinking locally and short term, and the British Communist Party throughout its life can be credited with an enormous contribution to the advance of the Labour and Trades Union movements, and inasmuch as I was a small cog in this big wheel I am a happy man. With a tinge of nostalgia I can recall the donkey work, making placards, preparing meetings, selling the *Daily Worker*, door-to-door canvassing, fly-posting, telephoning, collecting money, travelling to demos and conferences and sitting through committee meetings in 'smoke-filled' rooms.

*

At college I was becoming more and more committed to union work. In my job as a teacher I was particularly concerned with a class of ex-secondary modern students taking 'O' level geography. In order to motivate them and interest them in the academic and examination side of the subject I laid emphasis on audio-visual aids and fieldwork. This meant organising trips at weekends and at Easter, and the proof of the pudding lay in the surprisingly good exam results. My political views and activities were known and it seemed to me that I had to establish a certain reputation in my profession to ride over the obvious antipathy that would otherwise arise. It made me good at my job! As it was I was given very good references in my application for a post in the Aberdeen College of Education for which I was shortlisted, interviewed in December 1961 and offered the post of lecturer in geography.

Top: Edinburgh Civil Defence underground bunker, 1984.
Bottom: Anti-Trident demonstration, Edinburgh, 1986.

Top: Anti-Trident demonstration, Coulport, 1986.
Bottom: My back to the camera with Stockbridge CND.

Top: With President Ortega of Nicaragua, Edinburgh.
Bottom: Supporting the miner's strike picket, Monktonhall, 1984.

Top: Addressing an anti-nuclear conference in Japan,1986.
Bottom: Presentation by the City of Edinburgh of the award of
Good Citizen of the Year, 1988.

Top: With President Ortega of Nicaragua, Edinburgh.
Bottom: Supporting the miner's strike picket, Monktonhall, 1984.

Top: Addressing an anti-nuclear conference in Japan,1986.
Bottom: Presentation by the City of Edinburgh of the award of
Good Citizen of the Year, 1988.

Chapter VI
The Sixties in Aberdeen

> National identity is a delicate and precarious
> mixture of shared symbols, happy accidents,
> evolutionary chaos, historical inheritance,
> genetic roulette, political interference, cultural
> hand-me-downs, economics, the weather,
> geology, sunspots, Iron Age migration patterns,
> religion, bus routes, taste, landscape, the Gulf
> Stream and investment decisions made in
> Delaware or Zurich.
>
> Steven Bayley
> *New Statesman*, September 12th, 1997

Moving from the leafy suburbs of Greater London to the
centre of Aberdeen, the Granite City some five hundred
and fifty miles to the North, marked a sea change in our
physical and cultural environment that looked more like
emigrating than moving. However, we knew that there
were plenty of jobs that we could go back to if necessary,
and the children were at their most moveable age, so
mobility wasn't a problem. We didn't feel as though we
were burning our boats. The Sixties is marked down in
most people's minds as the decade of change with a youth
culture, a sexual revolution and the flowering of ideas in

fashion and lifestyles. For me, it was a decade of intense political involvement, of family life and my assimilation into another nation.

Our image of Scotland in general, and that of Aberdeen in particular, had been coloured by the media, although I knew something about its geography. Mary and I had also been on holiday on the West Coast, but separately as this was before we had actually met. We were typically English in our estimations of it – mountains and lochs, shipyards and coal, sheep and fish, bagpipes and haggis, Hogmanay and heather, ceilidhs and whisky – the familiar montage that still remains as the image of Scotland in so many people's minds today. I had also met some people from Scotland at sea, in political conferences and in education, but I knew better than to generalise from the characteristics of people away from home, especially 'expats'.

At my first school in Middlesex, Ruislip Manor, the art teacher was a Mr Simpson, who never seemed to have enough money on a Friday to pay for the week's tea money in the staff room, but I never supported my colleagues' remarks that 'All Scotsmen are mean...' For Aberdeen, in particular, there are numerous jokes, like the Aberdeen taxi that crashed and twenty-two passengers got out unhurt!

Aberdeen also has the reputation of being parochial, and indeed it was until the oil boom made it a cosmopolitan city. The local paper, the *Aberdeen Press and Journal* that has a bigger local circulation than all the other newspapers put together, still regards international news with some ambivalence. At the time of the sinking of the *Titanic* the headline on the front page was 'Aberdeen man drowned in boating accident'!

In the political arena I thought that the Scots made the best contributions, and reflected a more advanced political culture than the one in which I had cut my teeth in the South of England. I was thirty-five and at the height of my capabilities, not so much ambitious as intensely forward-looking, whether domestically, professionally or politically. I was amused by the local accent and the 'Doric', a north-east dialect with 'loons and quines' (lads and lassies), 'yer ken' (you know), 'fit like?' (how are you?), 'puddocks and horny gollocks' (frogs and earwigs) and a thousand others. I was also being made aware of a different sense of community and culture, stemming from a different history. The different legal system was obvious as soon as we negotiated the purchase of our house in Great Western Road. In England, either party can withdraw from the sale until written contracts have been exchanged and signed, and we were let down by the first buyer and had to put the house up for sale again. Meanwhile, in Scotland, a verbal agreement is a contract so we had two houses for a brief spell! Of all the hundreds of differences in the law, I think the vast majority are better in Scotland, particularly because they are based on the 'good of the community' rather than the property rights of the aristocracy as in England. What I immediately liked about Scotland was its variety, not just of landscape but of people. As Brian Groom describes them (*New Statesman*, August 1st, 1997), 'So talented yet so truculent, so adventurous yet so parochial. So vociferous yet so strangely compliant.' I would sum it up more succinctly as unity in diversity.

I swatted up the details of the different educational system I was now to engage in, but I had underestimated the implications. At least I had found an intelligible system, as against the absence of a system in England. One of the biggest cultural differences was one that is still wrongly perceived in England – that of the national aspirations. So often is it portrayed as national chauvinism, or more critically as the 'whinging Scots' when, at base, it is a question of democracy and the right of all peoples to have a say in deciding their own future rather than having this imposed against their will. People in England would only understand this burning frustration if the Westminster Parliament was dissolved and they were governed totally by Brussels.

Here, in Scotland, we have a secretary of state, accountable only to the prime minister in London who appointed him, having the power to go roughshod over the opinions of the majority and imposing his own, heading a Scottish Office employing fifteen thousand with a budget of fifteen billion pounds, appointing over one hundred and sixty quangos and giving only five billion pounds to the local authorities over which he exercises his right to intervene and limit their activities. Hence the 'Claim of Right' and the movement for a Scottish Parliament, which was only later to develop a profile demanding the recognition it deserved, forcing a Labour Government to take action.

One cannot overestimate the significance of the current proposals, obtained after years of campaigning, for a Parliament in Scotland radically different from that of Westminster. It will involve proportional representation, a gender balance, normal working hours, committees with executive powers, consensual rather than a confrontational style of politics and weight given to the recommendations of non-governmental organisations. Unless spokes are put in the wheel of change by English nationalists, its influence will spark off constitutional changes south of the border as well.

It was Harold Wilson who said that a week in politics is a long time, but it seems to me that the converse is also true. The development of an idea whose time has come sometimes takes a long time to incubate, filter through the population and get acted on by the decision-makers. Hence the role of civic society and its organisations and the activists who campaign on their behalf. I therefore look back with pride at the role I played in the sixties in the Aberdeen Peace Council, Peace Festivals and especially in the Committee for Peace in Vietnam with its lobbies to Parliament, demonstrations, letter writing, fund-raising for medical aid and ceaseless work in committee. Being in a position of responsibility it was far from boring and I gained much from the intense dialogue and years of concerted action with stalwarts like Dr Malcolm Pittock, Mary Klopper, the Synge family, Sadie ElSarrag, Owen Dudley Edwards and a host of others.

*

Shortly after my arrival in Aberdeen the Cuban crisis broke out and the threat of nuclear war between the superpowers was very real. The United States could no longer rule Cuba by proxy in order to further its economic and political interests. Fidel Castro nationalised the sugar industry and aimed at getting resources redeployed into health and education in order to relieve the abject poverty, especially in the rural areas. America blockaded and attempted the overthrow of Castro's government, declaring that Cuba lay in its sphere of influence and therefore had no right to nationalise American companies. At this time Castro was not a communist, but he was forced to trade and get help from the Soviet Union, with agreements to exchange sugar for oil and military support to defend himself. In 1962 America declared a total blockade of Cuba as a Russian convoy was crossing the Atlantic and missiles were identified on the decks of some of the ships. Kruschev declared that America's action was illegal under international law. The ships were not armed and must be allowed passage in international waters. American warships went to intercept the convoy and halt its passage by any means available and the Russians insisted that the ships were to proceed to Cuba. A clash on the high seas would quickly escalate into nuclear confrontation. The American submarines and supply ship left the Holy Loch. The British armed services were put on full alert. The convoy was approaching the ring of American warships. I joined the biggest and most representative protest march that Aberdeen had ever seen, with a flood of banners along Union Street urging, 'Hands off Cuba'.

I wrote to my MP, hoping the letter would arrive in time. The confrontation was timed for three o'clock in the afternoon of what I seem to recollect as a Tuesday. The day was calm and sunny, yet a thick gloom pervaded everything and everybody, including the media. Suddenly it was announced that the convoy had turned back and was heading for the Black Sea ports from whence it came. The headlines declared that the Soviet Union had been defeated by calling its bluff. America showed itself to be invincible. Castro would fall – as the press has been predicting for the last half century.

The agreement between Kennedy and Kruschev was that Russian missiles would be withdrawn from Cuba immediately and America would not invade. This in itself was all that Russia and Cuba wanted, but, in order that Kennedy got domestic support not to invade Cuba, Russia had also agreed to keep secret the American agreement to remove its missiles from the Turkish border which threatened the Soviet Union. This was projected as a defeat for Russia by all the media rejecting reports of the deal. That is, except the *Morning Star* whose readers were the only one privileged with the truth as on so many other occasions. Now, thirty-five years later, Geoffrey Hodgson who was then Washington correspondent of the *Observer* is able to reveal in the *New Statesman* (24/10/97) that 'With cheerful ruthlessness Kennedy leaked that it was only Adlai Stevenson – his defeated rival for the Democratic nomination – who had wanted a deal. Henceforth, any suggestion that there had been one could be dismissed as the ravings of the soft-on-communism left.' I have found that it is this type of manipulation of and by the media that is one of the most potent causes of the cynicism permeating today's electorate. Locally, one result of the Cuban crisis was a wider list of contacts and support for CND and the Peace Council. I therefore quickly got to know who were the main defenders in Aberdeen of these issues of world peace. I also found that communists played a leading role in the unions and the peace movement as well as in their own highly respected party organisation.

The day I arrived in Aberdeen I went to introduce myself to the area secretary, whose address I had previously obtained in order to get some general contextual information about the political scene. I met Margaret Rose at Maberly House, near the centre and a stone's throw from the college. She was very hospitable, enthusiastic and knowledgeable, running her house as a working men's hostel and with an office and meeting room in a large shed at the back, well-known as the party headquarters for north-east Scotland with its four hundred members.

There were about a dozen branches, some industrial like the transport (buses) and rails branches, others based on the locality such as the election wards of Mastrick and Northfields. All the information was at Maberly House. A handful of members did not want their identity disseminated, but there were no 'open' and 'closed' lists as I remember hearing about before the war. There was always the possibility of MI5 infiltration and this occurred at higher levels; for many years the London office was bugged, until it was discovered during redecoration. It was never a problem except on tactical grounds as our attitude was that if anyone joined and made a contribution in energy or finance he or she would be very welcome.

We were never engaged in any other than legitimate political campaigning but certain members had to have their anonymity respected in order to avoid threats to their livelihood. Whether or not people agreed with the politics, the Communist Party and individual members were well respected locally, despite the terrible lies, innuendoes and attacks nationally. I remember a colleague with whom I engaged in quite serious discussion during coffee and lunch breaks. He approached me with a different question every day and sympathised with the answers. He then asked me if I was a member of the Labour Party, one of the many Trotskyite groups, and continued down a list. He then said I should join something instead of keeping my ideas to myself, to which I finally told him I was in the Communist Party. 'Anything but that! What are people going to think of me if they see me talking to you?' and we never held a conversation again. Such was the guilt by association that the establishment cultivated with respect to the CPGB, but, of course, from their point of view it was the only real challenge to the perpetuation of their privilege and power.

My privilege was being associated with so many outstanding human beings devoted to the betterment of others less fortunate, such as Bob Cooney of the International Brigade in Spain, John Bacon, a scientist, May Balnaves, a lecturer in English, Jimmy Oats, teacher and union man, Jimmy Milne, who became one of the best general secretaries of the STUC, Bill Henderson, painter and decorator, Andy Smith and the campaign against joining the Common Market, Sid English, the Lennox family, the Thomson family and Norrie Williamson, who accompanied me countless times selling the *Daily Worker/Morning Star* and who died suddenly of a heart attack after standing for many hours collecting for medical aid for Vietnam on a cold, wet and windy Saturday in Union Street.

It would be boring to add to the list, but there were many many others beavering away at a local level, without any reward for themselves save the satisfaction of tackling injustice, poverty, ignorance and the misery inflicted by the jungle warfare of capitalism where the devil takes the hindmost. There were, of course, those who chose to leave the Party and advance themselves as they could not do by remaining inside, but who can blame them?

The social side was also well developed, with many of the Scottish traditional singing, dancing and drinking sessions, but I didn't take part and I was thought of as a bit of a loner and even unsociable, but I was keen to return home and to Mary and the children, as I knew they didn't appreciate my frequent absences. I looked on the Party as being more important than my pleasures and welfare, but others may have thought that this subservience to 'good causes' should only come second to devotion to one's family.

There was one particular episode in the annals of the Party history of Aberdeen which I felt it to be my unpleasant duty to act upon. The area secretary, Margaret Rose, had no more diligent assistant than myself. She was a tireless worker too. We drafted leaflets, bulletins, news sheets and letters, replicating them on the Gestetner. I was instrumental in drafting and distributing a powerful one on comprehensive education which was widely distributed. Material for meetings of the branch and area was prepared, including proposals for action that had been decided at the Scottish Committee. Democratic centralism was the key principle underlying the work and organisation of the Party, whereby discussions on all issues were discussed at all levels, representatives were elected to the next level in the hierarchy and decisions at a higher level subsumed those at a lower one. In theory it was democratic. Every member could say what they wanted to say and they did. It was centralist inasmuch as decisions on policy and action were handed down in order to get things done in a unified and concerted manner as effectively as possible. The Party was not a talking shop.

Margaret Rose was a powerful character, and her goal was to get policy implemented as quickly as possible, but she became intolerant of those who didn't see things her way. A few years passed and I became uneasy at her unwarranted criticism and even condemnation of those with whom she did not see eye to eye. An increasing number of members avoided her, and at first I defended her as the key worker, volunteering to do all the day-to-day work. Finally, I put the situation in front of her. She not only insisted on the opposite but her ego trips were extended, and I wrote a long and detailed letter to Gordon McLennan, then Scottish Secretary, proposing her removal and, in order not to be accused of going behind her back I sent her a copy.

The storm that followed led to her eventual resignation. We no longer had use of her premises. With the help of loans from two other comrades I bought, on behalf of the Party, a shop at 21 Urquhart Road, and a group of us furnished and equipped it and reinvigorated the membership at a time of difficult political circumstances, but in our view action was no less urgent.

To the outside world who listened to the continuous anti-communist propaganda we were mere agents of Moscow. For a long time differences with the CPSU were not expressed outside the Party as that would have given fuel to the non-stop crusade against us by blowing up stories of splits and dissent and causing disarray in the party. Actually, as long ago as 1951 the *British Road to Socialism* spelt out the parliamentary road to socialism replacing 'the crises, insecurity, profiteering, inequalities and social antagonisms of capitalist society'. The differing views of the British delegation to the 1964 International Conference of Communist Parties were accepted as valid points of view by the CPSU. The CPGB was particularly concerned at the action taken against dissidents and questions of inner party democracy in the Soviet Union, but we accepted the leading role played by the Soviet Union as the only way to defend socialism wherever it was achieved in the world.

Soviet ships regularly visited Aberdeen from Murmansk and Archangel to unload timber. Occasionally, some of us visited them, were shown around and chatted to whoever spoke some English. They could go ashore but had no convertible currency to buy sterling so they could only window-shop, unlike the Polish crews who would be seen bartering and buying for their home market. The morning after a casual visit to a Soviet ship, there was a phone call from the captain stating that one of their sailors had not returned the previous evening and that the police had denied any knowledge of his whereabouts. We went down to the ship, phoned the police HQ and got nowhere.

To cut a long story short, the sailor was brought back four days later by the police and dropped off at the foot of the gangway. He was an eighteen year old on his first voyage, had lost his way back to ship, knew no English and had stopped a police car. Having been indoctrinated to think that 'Russians want to escape', they took him to Craiginches Prison for interview, but it was a bank holiday weekend in England and the Home Office Russian-speaking official was not available. There was, of course, a Russian department at the university, and also teachers of Russian in the schools, but the police had instructions to deny everything until the Home Office had dealt with it. Yet, in Britain, we are supposed to know who the police are holding.

Another such denial of human rights occurred when a well-known Irish psychiatrist, whom I heard speak about the denial of the right to work, council houses and jobs to Catholics in Derry. This was before 'Bloody Sunday', when British troops fired and killed over a dozen of them in a peaceful demonstration. She was arrested on suspicion of harbouring an IRA suspect in her large house in the Midlands where she was well-known for giving hospitality. All her activities were open for anyone to see. She was publicly critical of the IRA and emphasised the political way forward as the only one to take. When I heard on the radio about her arrest I was taken aback and wrote to all I could. I supported the campaign for her release as she was being kept indefinitely in prison without charge. After several months she was released, but her job had been given to someone else and her private life was devastated. Ninety-two per cent of the 7,397 people held under the Prevention of Terrorism Act between 1972 and 1992 were never charged, and many who were charged were released after many years when their innocence was finally proved. How many more examples of miscarriages of justice have I got to give, even from my limited experience, before we question the closed nature of our society – the 'Free World'?

However, the injustices of capitalism don't make the injustices under socialist regimes excusable. At first, we called it 'enemy propaganda'. Then it was the 'growing pains' of a new system under threat. I tended to say that it was a continuation of the previous regime's well-tried methods that were part of the culture, but I heard no one defend Stalin's crimes. These revelations were a shock to us all but they were nothing to do with socialism. Some comrades left the Communist Party, viewing human nature in more glowing terms than others, including myself, who tried to differentiate between what the present situation was, a complex mixture of the good and the bad, and what we wanted it to be.

The shake-out began after Hungary in 1956, and especially after our open disagreement with the CPSU over Czechoslovakia in 1968. The *Morning Star*, reflecting the views of the Executive Committee of the CPGB, became ever more critical of the CPSU and this led to the hijacking of the paper by its editorial staff and breakaways from the Party such as the New Communist Party.

I kept to the mainstream and was loyal to the end but never uncritical. It just seemed to me that the political situation always demanded a movement that campaigned on the key issues of the moment. The Communist Party was the most effective organisation trying to do this, if it could avoid the dogmatism and sectarianism that had been self-defeating in the past. Also it had to avoid the revisionism and reformism that had led all Labour organisations to end up trying to make capitalism work better than the Tories, with the inevitable consequence of furthering the interests of the wealthy lest they move their capital abroad. This, in turn, meant reducing public expenditure and making the poor poorer. The 'trickle down' theory, whereby the wealthy would be able to spend even more, pushing up employment, was given as a justification but has never been shown to work in practice. More likely are the extra funds invested abroad.

*

The post of lecturer in geography was to start on April 1st, 1962, but I had already organised an educational tour to Warsaw and Moscow for the Easter holidays, having circulated union members in Surrey. There were over forty applications and although it was tailor-made for us it was organised through Progressive Tours, the only company at that time with tours to the Soviet Union. I was used to putting as much detail as possible on paper beforehand when taking students away on fieldwork, leaving nothing to chance or hearsay, and I circulated these tour members similarly, using the twenty-four hour clock: '1900 Assemble at the departure gate, Liverpool Street Station for the 1930 train etc.' I waited anxiously for two people who never arrived. We travelled via the Hook of

Holland by overnight train, and then through Berlin, but at every border we were woken up to produce passports.

Passing from West to East Germany was more tedious, but Progressive Tours had already sent the passenger list for visas so I found a welcoming official and I gave the names of our absentees. The train had then to pass through a West German station, but it was not a scheduled stop. Even so, one of our missing friends was there having taken the plane. He said that the other person, who happened to have been my previous headmistress, had mistaken 1900 hrs. for 9 p.m. and was catching the next train to Warsaw. At the next checkpoint on the other side of Berlin I told the immigration officials and our missing friend told us in Warsaw that she had experienced no border problems as she was apparently already known to them at every control point!

At a time when all references to the Eastern bloc were tarred with the same brush, it surprised people to see such contrasts between and within the different countries there. In Poland, the guard and officials were in a compartment at the end of the carriage drinking vodka. In the Soviet Union, the carriages and dining car were continually being cleaned and 'stakhans' of tea brought round. The farming landscape changed radically from East Germany's collective farms and tractors to Poland's smallholdings and horse-drawn ploughs and then back to the large fields, lakes and forests of Byelorussia.

We spent a day in schools and sightseeing in Warsaw which I had intended as a break from the long journey, but it was enough to get people talking about it for some time after. The real objective was Moscow and I subsequently wrote articles about the educational system as I saw it. I started by explaining that it was not so much communist as continental, and that the ingredients were a mixture of history, ideology, pragmatism and individual initiatives, with resources that suggested a priority being given to the raising of standards across the board.

It would be easy to say now that my glasses were rose-tinted, but I was also conscious that there had to be a countervailing influence against the unremitting attacks on all aspects of Soviet life which imbued most of the population of the West with a very warped and, indeed, demonstrably outrageous view of the facts. It was certainly the case that although everything was new to me it wasn't *news* to me. I was not taken by surprise and shaken abruptly as some of my colleagues were, who had to change some of their cherished opinions while at the same time using the 'exceptions' clause, 'We were only shown the best...', in order to try to accommodate the incongruities between what they had read and what they had experienced. In other words, who had been previously brainwashed, me or them?

*

It was literally the day after arriving back in Aberdeen that I started my new job. The College of Education was referred to as the TC – the Training College of long standing with its origins in the Church of Scotland. Its constitution was now changed as well as its name, with a board of governors appointed by the secretary of state and a board of studies of all the lecturing staff. Existing staff had been to school in Aberdeen, the University of Aberdeen, teaching posts in Aberdeen or the region and had been appointed via advertisements in the *Aberdeen Press and Journal*. In 1961 a 'foreigner' from Glasgow had been appointed principal, and he brought with him a cohort of Glaswegians as principal lecturers to expand their departments. For the first time adverts went into the *Times Educational Supplement* with all-British coverage, and that's where I came in with several others.

Academic education had a status in the population of Scotland that was way above that in England. However, geography teaching in England had been developing much more rapidly as it was based on earlier specialisation, whereas in Scotland a teacher of English usually taught history and geography as subsidiaries, especially in the junior secondary schools and lower forms of the senior secondaries, and the syllabuses and methods had not progressed as quickly as in England.

University geography departments in England and Scotland were, however, advancing in parallel, and school exam syllabuses were now changing for the better. In this situation I found that with my experience in fieldwork for pupils and use of audio-visual aids I was able to make a particular contribution, especially with the training year of the increasing number of honours graduates that the university was now producing.

The principal, Jimmy Scotland, was very effective, especially in his public relations. He was also a playwright, producer and actor and his extrovert nature made his chairmanship of the board of studies interesting, if not entertaining. I was rather apprehensive at making any contribution. I was afraid that I wouldn't express myself adequately, but I did venture to suggest from my experience in a further education college that ringing bells every forty-five minutes was unnecessary, and gave the place an atmosphere of school instead of an institution of higher learning. There was blank amazement from the many who had not been accustomed to anything else and a debate followed resulting in a trial week. There were no more bells. Everybody had a watch, fears of classes arriving late disappeared and it soon became a forgotten phenomenon which made one wonder why it had not been disposed of before. The same happened to the wearing of academic gowns and other formalities, but the sign of the times was most importantly witnessed in a debate on whether religious instruction should be compulsory for all students.

A group of us put the motion down on the agenda and what followed seemed like a re-run of the nineteenth century debate between Bishop Wilberforce and Huxley. True that RI was compulsory in the schools. True that the Church of Scotland was the only denomination allocated a place on the governing body. True that some theologians saw compulsion as self-defeating and wanted only committed Christians to specialise in its teaching. But the lines were very markedly drawn in the debate and it was left to the principal to work it out for a future date.

In order to make my position and promotion prospects more secure I enrolled at the University of Aberdeen for the Dip.Ed. and then the M.Ed. courses. This involved lectures from 4 to 6 p.m. on three evenings per week for three years, in addition to a heavy load of essays and study. In the fourth year I completed a research thesis on 'Staying on at School', using the schools in Aberdeen. Now, in the Nineties, more than seventy per cent of Scottish school students (formerly called pupils) stay on after the leaving age of sixteen under a comprehensive system, and we forget that in the Sixties the figure was less than twenty-five per cent under the selective system of senior and junior secondary schools.

One of the findings of my study was the crucial importance of the head teacher in accounting for the differences in staying on. For example, Bill Christie at Summerhill Junior Secondary had introduced certificate courses and ran a variety of after-school activities, with a much bigger proportion staying on than at Northfield, which had a similar socio-economic catchment area. As a matter of interest, Christie was followed by R.F. Mackenzie from Braehead in Fife, and he turned the school into quite a different direction, with its main emphasis on education for leisure and making school a much more attractive place for the less able. R.F. Mackenzie stated in his subsequent book, *The Unbowed Head*, that society as organised at present is a jungle. 'It has clearings of caring people here and there, but the pattern isn't one of caring. We are entering the dark days,' he insisted. 'The "Ode to Joy" is postponed.' He said it was essential to change society by starting with the young citizens of tomorrow as the only hope for the future. In my opinion he seemed to have forgotten that the whole of the educational system is devised to perpetuate the present society and its needs. Parents and employers were looking to the employment prospects of school leavers.

This radical change of emphasis from academic work to leisure activities divided the staff, led to public debate and accusations and eventually to his suspension and dismissal. I had the opportunity to discuss some of his ideas with him as a visiting lecturer from the college. I admired his caring attitude for the generally neglected majority of our children, but I had also admired Christie's determination to give as many as possible a chance to climb the educational ladder, and the way he went out and about the corridors, classrooms and playground, meeting and encouraging students and staff rather than staying in his room and administering from a distance.

Both factions denied that there could be two different approaches operating in the same school, but that was before comprehensive education was implemented to do just that. Comprehensive education was not a panacea for the ills of society in which there are conflicting interests not capable of being satisfied. It is of interest to me that in contrast to the English situation, three decades later, there were no movements in Scotland to reverse the process or to 'opt out', so how did the changes come about in the first place?

In the wider community comprehensive education was being discussed at a political level, and I was closely in touch with Councillor Bob Hughes (later to be the local Member of Parliament) and the various memos that were being circulated. The Labour Government was keen on its introduction, but there was often a hybrid type being implemented by local authorities as a compromise solution.

In Aberdeen at that time, twenty-two per cent went to senior secondaries and courses leading to external examinations. At Aberdeen Grammar School a proportion of the pupils were admitted at the age of five after passing a test and paying a fee, but with no eleven plus to bar their way to the secondary part of the school. By this time I was taking the M.Ed. course part-time at the university, and I was well versed in much of the literature on comprehensive education, especially that by Professor Brian Simon of Leicester University, who was a recognised and influential authority and also incidentally, a member of the Communist Party. I once invited him up as a speaker.

I attended many of the meetings on the topic, no matter who organised them. At first I held my fire. I was still rather reticent, but then found that it was far better for me to prepare my contribution and get in first, as it would set the scene and make it far harder for the chairman to ignore what I had to say by invoking the time element. I also learned the technique of starting by getting the sympathy of the audience – 'Many of us would agree that... but are concerned that...'

There was one particular meeting at which the chief education officer was speaking, at a time when the Labour councillors were proposing comprehensive schools from eleven to eighteen, and I had information that the chief education officer sympathised with the conservative group in opposing them, but his public utterances talked of educating every child to the maximum of his or her potential. I also knew he was proposing a compromise of selection at thirteen instead of eleven, and of the sixth-form college idea. Research by Eggleston and others had shown that schools with an upper limit of sixteen led to a good proportion of able working-class children not moving on to the sixth-form college.

The director's speech included the Labour group's proposals as he was loyally bound to do, being employed as a servant of the council, but he then raised the objections saying that 'other' experts had suggested alternatives. He then gave the necessary details with a strong hint that those would command the greatest degree of public support. I was well prepared and faced him head-on with what HE thought and was trying to achieve, namely the perpetuation of the outmoded selective system we had at the present. I also anticipated his reply that there were administrative and financial problems to the Labour proposals and explained why he and his friends were keen to defeat the proposals, and laid bare the tactics he was using now that he realised that the *status quo* was untenable. He was visibly taken aback, and the hall reverberated with muffled murmurings and the turning of heads. The chairman rapidly moved on to the next question.

I doubt whether I should have been so outspoken, especially when I similarly opposed what the college principal had said at a big conference on the topic, even though I took the precaution of not mentioning him personally. I had also organised a letter to the *Press and Journal* signed by about thirty of the lecturing staff, declaring that the *status quo* was no longer serving us well and proposing the comprehensive alternative. It appeared on the front page and annoyed the principal, even though we had signed in our personal capacities.

My colleague, May Balnaves, told me how I was jeopardising my prospects for promotion and later a friend on the governing body brought up the question of my discrimination after hearing the principal's remarks that my politics made me unsuitable for a post of higher responsibility.

I think it was ironic therefore that some years later, when the opportunity again arose, no voices were raised in a similar manner. I say 'ironic' because had there been genuine objections to my promotion they may have been suspected of being a cover for unacceptable political objections! Of course, I think that I had been worthy of promotion the first time round! More importantly, Aberdeen went ahead with a fully comprehensive system from eleven to eighteen.

★

My work at the College of Education was a source of great pleasure and satisfaction for me. Geography was my first love. I looked upon it as 'Human Ecology' – the complex interaction of human and physical factors, each of which had to be studied both separately and together, but I could not study it without regard to its dissemination, and therefore teaching was, as it were, my second love, and it has been my good fortune to have been doing both, albeit part-time, until I was seventy.

It may sound a little arrogant, but I would consider my life to have been worthwhile had I done nothing other than teaching, so that it may seem a little strange that its elucidation is not featuring in these memoirs. This is because this base has got to be assumed as a vocation and it was the way I earned my living that enabled me to do everything else. My career has gone the way I wanted and hoped, desiring none other.

This is patently not because I could do no other. I could have gone back to a successful career at sea. After early retirement I was happy teaching English as a foreign language in France for a while. I was very successful designing and selling kitchens for five years – success in this case being measured in American style by the amount of financial reward.

If these were the only considerations, the title of these memoirs, *One Step Forward, Two Steps Back*, should be reversed. I have marched forwards rather than backwards. I have felt and seen the positive results of my academic career, although I accept that all teachers give themselves credit for their successes and ascribe other reasons for their failures. No, this is not the main issue, but only a contributory factor in the making of 'a left-wing activist', contributory inasmuch as it was background to my interest, knowledge and commitment to global problems, and was reflected in the need for local action.

Similarly, my home and family life, ongoing and changing as it has been, is significant here to the extent it has both helped and hindered my conviction that individuals have got to stand up and be counted in the movement to defend the interests of the vast majority against the unrelenting downward pressure from a rich, greedy and power-hungry minority. Because it was an intellectual conviction rather than a psychological need for me to be involved, I had to convince and pressure myself to take action. This might even seem absurd to those who have labelled me as a 'doer' rather than a 'thinker'. It helps to have the capacity for hard work, the health to carry on for long periods, the determination to see things through to the end, but I drove myself from conviction, sometimes against what I would have liked to have done for short-term advantage, and therefore it was always just as easy to relax, change activity, move on or do nothing, like the chap who just sat and thought, and sometimes just sat!

Yes, it is so easy to take the line of least resistance, and it may unfortunately be the case that each generation has to learn afresh the problems of living together and how to respond to them. A sophisticated education may help the individual to contribute to the collective conscience, but one cannot be optimistic that human misery can be removed on the scale that is necessary. It may well be that catastrophes, not too small to be ignored and not too big as to be overwhelming, will have to occur before whole peoples are galvanised into action.

It seemed to me that my biggest problem was not myself, although we all have a habit of deluding ourselves when it is convenient to do so, but rather persuading those who professed that they wanted change to move themselves out of their armchairs. My approach was to persuade if I could, compromise if I must and leave alone if they opposed.

In my attempts to get some commitment and action, those with families who were often convinced but 'had neither time nor money' I sympathised with, but older people seemed to have, in my humble opinion, a disproportionate say in the decision-making process. I therefore resolved not to make excuses on my own behalf in order to lighten my load. Young people were more in evidence voicing their political opinions in the Sixties and Seventies than in the remaining part of the century, but they tended to move on to other locations, interests and jobs. Yet their enthusiasm and creative abilities were not only welcome but seen as the basis of the future of any movement or organisation and therefore had to be given support wherever possible. It also meant the occasional paying of their debts as occurred when the YCL booked a hall and a film projector but was unable to pay the bill.

Through necessity I had compartmentalised my life as I played the different roles of a political organiser in the Party and as secretary for many years of the Committee for Peace in Vietnam and the Aberdeen Peace Council, as lecturer in geography and especially that of father and husband.

Unfortunately, I found it difficult, if not impossible, to discuss the complexities of my style of life with Mary. Her views were black or white, whereas I saw various shades of grey and inherent contradictions in the way we have to deal with people in the wider world and in the longer term. Nevertheless, despite all the hours given to campaigning, working, studying and attending meetings and conferences we did have a shared existence at home with the children, in the garden, visiting friends and relatives, some social evenings and on holiday, including a couple of visits to the Soviet Union.

I accept that she saw my outside interests as a 'left-wing activist' as abnormal compared with the 'norms' portrayed in all the soaps and women's magazines. Mary was very conventional in all her opinions and behaviour and held that a family man should be working or at home. It is difficult to argue against this attitude and it therefore says a lot for her that she helped me with fund-raising bazaars and jumble sales. I was known to rush away home after every meeting or event rather than join the others in a drink and a chat, but I was keen to compensate for my absence by helping her in the house and seeing the children each evening and at weekends. It may not be too frivolous to add that I spent a lot more time with my children than the eleven minutes that the average father spent each day according to the research of Gershunny in *Demography*, 1968.

I had intended this *modus vivendi* to last a lifetime, but I had not sufficiently realised that relationships change anyway, either widening and deepening or drifting, cooling and becoming routinely boring. An effort has got to be made to mature and to change a relationship in the direction mutually desirable, not necessarily facing each other as facing in the same direction in order to jump life's hurdles together.

Thus we found moving house stimulating rather than traumatising. Our first house in Aberdeen was an eight-roomed Victorian detached house at 127 Great Western Road, standing well back from the road with a sizeable garden. Redecorating, shopping for carpets and planning the garden together were immensely pleasurable activities.

There was a self-contained flat upstairs which we let rent-free to Rhona and her husband who had an unskilled job on the railways, in exchange for housework and babysitting. Unfortunately, we discovered dry rot and we brought in Rentokil who almost demolished one part of the house as they followed through the fungus from one granite block to another. We took out a second mortgage, but our subsequent unease and lack of funds in the bank forced us to move not far away to a large and beautiful upstairs flat at 69 Fountainhall Road, in the heart of the West End. Built towards the end of the nineteenth century of Rubislaw granite, it had been divided and modernised so that it combined the grandeur of former times with the easily kept modern amenities and decor. The *pièce de résistance* was the primrose-coloured bath in the middle of a large room which should have been photographed for *Homes and Gardens*! The small shared garden was not really adequate, but I regularly took the children to the nearby Duthie Park to feed the ducks.

One evening, when we had colleagues for a meal, we had a frying-pan fire which blackened the kitchen. There were no smoke alarms then. Shortly after that the washing machine flooded the flat below. I negotiated the repairs through the insurance, but Mary was too embarrassed to meet the neighbours so she decided she would no longer be happy there and wanted to move to the country.

We found, or rather bought, a large old house next to the Ythan Hotel in Newburgh, ten miles north of Aberdeen within easy commuting distance of both our places of work. It had three storeys with seven small rooms and a long garden down to the river, with a footbridge over to the golf course, recreation grounds and sand dunes. We had money left over from the conveyancing and installed oil-fired central heating and made considerable alterations including a large double-glazed picture window on the second floor back room overlooking the superb landscape of the Ythan estuary.

Walks across the links were exhilarating whatever the season, but I had decided that I would never have the time to play golf and, although I was tempted, I never bought any clubs nor borrowed any in order to 'have a go'. Nobody I knew in Scotland understood nor appreciated these remarks, so common is it to take up golf. John played football with Pip and his other primary school friends on the 'rekky'. One Christmas I bought a small inflatable, only just big enough for John and myself to paddle along in the stream as the tide rose to cover the boulders and mud. Mr Shewan, an elderly man, looked after the golf house and befriended children and adults alike, so that he often came across to see the children back from the local school before Mary and I arrived back home. Two decades later Sandra and John accused him of sexual abuse, but by now he was dead and buried and they opted to see a therapist rather than discuss it with anybody else. I respect their wishes for confidentiality, so I have been unable to disentangle the facts and the role played by a possible false memory syndrome. Details apart, both Mary and I are annoyed at having had no suspicions nor reasons to doubt his integrity, but whether or not we were naive it was our responsibility and not that of the children.

Mary was much more integrated into village life than I was. In fact, for me it was a dormitory village, but Mary found it well to her liking and made many friends and acquaintances. One year we had my brother John, Bernice and their four children from Canada visit us, and I hired a Dormobile to take everybody around, including a trip to Skye and down south to my parents and Sybil. Everything seemed to be jogging along fine with Mary and we were determined that this was to be our last move; but we had, of course, always thought the same – when we purchased our first house in Greenford, then at Caterham, at Great Western Road, Fountainhall Road and finally now at 'Ocean View', Newburgh.

Mary and I had few mutual friends, but she accompanied me to evening meals with my colleagues and I helped her to entertain the friends she invited to the house. I tended to limit my friendships to the role they played in my life whether professional, political or as a neighbour. One particular colleague, Frank Whittaker, became a close friend, but he died of lung cancer a few years later.

He first approached me at an Advisory Committee on Education in Glasgow, as he had applied for a post in the primary education department at the college. He had been in the coal mines and then the forces, followed by emergency training to be a teacher, like myself, but he didn't subsequently take a degree.

He became a head teacher of a small school in Fife, and it amused me to hear comments which were effectively challenging his ability to train primary school teachers from colleagues who had never been outside the academic system. His wife had been secretary to John Gollan many years previously, and he was particularly keen to discuss and work for a change to a comprehensive system for schools.

He was the life and soul of any social gathering, with an enormous repertoire of Scottish ballads. He then decided on an Open University course in geography and geology, for which he frequently asked my advice and help and accompanied me on two occasions with the B.Ed. advanced group on fieldwork to the Yorkshire Dales. He died in his fifties, shortly after having been awarded an honours degree in geography, and I couldn't help asking myself the unanswerable question – why him?

*

The Sixties have become known historically for the sexual revolution that is supposed to have occurred. There was no doubt that a teenage culture was in full flow. Young people had buying power. Consumer goods were now being produced in abundance and they needed markets. Advertisers seized on this easy marketing of such things as fashion clothes, records, Coke and entertainment. Young people worked or got reasonable student grants. The dating game was more obvious and premarital sex was unashamedly discussed. Students particularly engaged in social and political issues, and took part in demonstrations on apartheid, women's lib, Rhodesia and especially Vietnam. Unlike today's students, who feel insecure and worried about their job prospects, those who qualified found work. They had the luxury to think of the world outside and the ability to question events around them. The traditional roles of men and women were changing, but why hadn't this happened earlier? Philip Larkin, the poet, said that sexual intercourse began in 1963, meaning, of course, that nobody talked frankly about it until then.

In fact, the word 'teenager' was only in current usage after Elvis Presley's number one hit 'Rock Around The Clock' in the late Fifties, being imported into Britain soon after. Demographically, the post-war baby boom became a teenage boom in the Sixties, so that there were more than a few different aspects giving young people prominence.

Much has been written about the Sixties – as though they registered a turning point in the evolution of British culture and politics. Was society disintegrating or was the deadwood of unwanted tradition being cut away? Were people more optimistic or pessimistic about the future? Did 'freedom' at last break out, with the casting aside of moral codes? What about The Beatles and the guitar-rich pop group culture? What about Carnaby Street and a new consumerism countered by flower power and opting out? Was there a recognition of a more pluralistic society and the rise of feminism and environmentalism? Where was Prime Minister Wilson's cutting edge of a white-hot technological revolution?

The redevelopment of many city centres, the pulling down of slum dwellings and the erection of concrete and glass tower blocks made visible a change in policy, ideas and particularly fashion. It seemed to me that it was probably a confused mix of different aspirations and also the result of the increased access to the immediacy of television, but I certainly caught hold of the change in attitudes from the wartime generation that 'made do', to a younger generation rejecting the prescriptions of their elders. It also seemed to me that Britain's role in the Cold War had a knock-on effect that led to a disillusionment and a cynicism that laid the basis for the advance of Thatcherism a decade later – but more momentous events happened to me meantime.

Chapter VII
The Seventies in France

> ...she would have me as a beast – not that, I
> being a beast, she would have me, but that she,
> being a very beastly creature, lays claim to me.
>
> *Comedy of Errors*, 3.2.86–88

There's nothing so constant as change, but in 1970 this was to be traumatic for all concerned. It resulted in my moving out to a rented room in Albert Street, Aberdeen. You know what I'm going to say, or you think you do. The history of literature, plays, films, television soaps and street gossip is full of it. Husband meets another woman. It's as simple as that – or is it? Whose story do you believe anyway? How can anyone be objective when they are deeply and emotionally involved? When passions run, interests clash, judgements confuse and trust disappears, what is there to pick up? The pages of history cannot be turned back but we can try and understand how they were turned over. Therefore, instead of a justification or a post-mortem I shall describe without explanation and then try to assess how much was positive in what to the outside world would be labelled a disaster, but perhaps, in retrospect, was one that was waiting to happen.

I was nominated to go to a conference in Berlin, and in recognition of my work in the peace movement there was a week's holiday at a trades union centre in Heringsdorf in the GDR. One evening a woman of my own age from France asked me, in 'franglais', to see some literature she had in her room. She closed the door and embraced me. This you won't believe; but I immediately reopened the door and took her to the bar and told her the usual happily married story. We exchanged comments and observations with my school French and her school English, which started to develop into the conversation I had never been able to have with Mary.

I repeat, the road to hell is paved with good intentions. I refused an invitation to go to bed with her, even though I dreamt about it, because I knew that it would have implications beyond my ability to imagine. She gave me a photo. I had nothing to give in return but promised to write. We parted after a passionate embrace and I wondered whether we would ever meet again; perhaps when the children had grown up? Such was my naive rationalisation, as though I could calculate such things in advance and on my own to arrange the course of events.

Back in Aberdeen I was taken aback at the daily arrival of her letters, c/o 21 Urquhart Road. If I had already let loose my imagination, Gisele's had run riot and I needed the aid of a French dictionary, as well as more time to think and respond, not every few months, but almost every day. It certainly inflated my ego. It was obvious to Mary that something was amiss and following a woman's intuition, she searched and found the photo. Now the whole world tumbled around us and she wouldn't even allow me to deny that I had deliberately not slept with her as I wanted to maintain my loyalty to her and the children.

A major crisis had suddenly broken and I suggested that we keep our cool and keep the children out of it until we had discussed it further and in the light of a new day. Mary concluded that the best course of action for her was to do exactly the opposite and spike my guns.

Pamela, then fifteen, was called down from her room, but I refrained from entering the discussion, as whatever I said was calculated to inflame the situation further. Naturally, at that late hour, nothing was agreed except that I would write and end it forthwith. Mary phoned around in desperation. Jean White, her friend and neighbour from across the road, invited me to talk it out with her. By a remarkable coincidence Jean knew me as a colleague in my first school twenty years earlier. I appreciated her comments on human relationships which gave me food for thought.

But the dice had been thrown. Trust had gone.

Mary was getting worse not better, and I was left in a vacuum that was deafening in its silence. Time passed, probably not as long as it seemed as I was experiencing it. Gisele eventually wrote in deep distress that I had not even given her the right of reply, and pleading for the maintenance of some sort of contact albeit only at long intervals. This was from the heart but inevitably the correspondence restarted via my college address. Mary and I tried at first to manage the situation.

When challenged, I replied to the effect that I would promise to stay with her for at least four years for the sake of the children, mistakenly thinking I was being helpful. She told me that if I wasn't going to keep my marriage vows I had better pack up there and then and never come back.

This was, of course, the logic of making sure it was not going to go my way, whether or not it was in her best interest. To cut out a possible five more chapters of the sequel, I rented a room, met Gisele during the holidays and consummated our terribly romantic and intense relationship. Being thrown into the deep end so suddenly caused enormous problems, but I was able to survive them, whereas Mary and the children were becoming submerged emotionally and it made me anxious and sad that I could find no answer that would satisfy them.

I made over the house and its contents to Mary and kept the car and my personal effects. I knew that Mary was still traumatised by our separation and that increased my feeling of guilt, especially as I saw no way of compensating for it. Against my lawyer's advice, I paid the maintenance she asked for as I was keen to keep the peace and to see the children on a regular basis, but so deep was her bitterness and hatred of Gisele that she made any excuse for me not to see them and I had to obtain a court order.

Gisele was, at first, reluctant to consider moving to Scotland, as her two teenage daughters were requiring a lot of attention where their studies and boyfriends were concerned, which she put down to the convulsions in the France of 1968 rather than the consequence of her marriage break-up. I unsuccessfully applied for posts in colleges in France and Switzerland to teach English as a foreign language, but I had not yet gained any qualifications to do so. Then Gisele was badly shaken in a car accident and obtained an invalidity pension from her primary teaching. She took classes to learn English and finally decided to move to Scotland with her fifteen year old son, Gilles, and seventeen year old daughter, Isabelle, who made one visit with her boyfriend and then returned to France with him to live in a village near Metz.

I had no money, but I bought a new house in both our names with a one hundred per cent mortgage. By arrangement with the builder I decorated it inside and out in return for a cashback which I spent on kitchen equipment. One year after we had first met we moved in with Gisele's furniture, and I only just managed to pay Clark and Rose out of my slim savings. It was an exciting, exhilarating and romantic first year, but every day was spent problem-solving questions of money, homesickness, language, children, travel and finally Gisele's health.

This was always a concern, but never more so than after yet another car accident by a hit-and-run motorist, who had neither road tax nor a licence. Gisele spent three months in hospital in Aberdeen. Would our relationship stand up to all this? To reassure her of my permanent intentions we got married in Ellon Registry Office and, amongst other things, we agreed that I pay for everything when we were in Scotland and she would pay when we were holidaying in France.

I got on well with her family – her daughters with their boyfriends in Metz, and her parents in the Massif Central, quite a contrast from Paris where we stayed with her sister in the luxurious top flat of the fire headquarters where he was the colonel. We exchanged houses with teachers in the South of France for three successive summers. Even though Gisele was a strong socialist supporter I found myself doing less, rather than more, political work: self-evident you might think if I told you even more about our travels to Italy, Egypt and Canada or about our new-found friends in the oil industry and the mutual pleasures of gardening.

It was perhaps also due to the change in the fortunes of the Communist Party as it became openly Eurocommunist, and the pro-Soviet *Morning Star* divorced itself from it; other factors to be taken into account were the end of the Vietnamese War and the general disillusionment with the Labour Government's implementation of right-wing policies and increasing confusion amongst the ideologues and young people alike.

At the time, all the signs were hopeful that the Left was gathering strength and I attended demonstrations in support of the UCS workers, who won their famous victory over closures, the successful miners strike of '74, and the students also took a leading role at protest meetings, vigils and marches for Peace in Vietnam. There were also militant movements in Europe and North America, so that we were optimistic in our view that socialist policies would eventually prevail – as these mass movements of ordinary people became politicised – and that the left within the Labour Party would eventually win the day.

There were always strong debates within the meetings of the membership of the Communist Party, especially after 1956, but no dirty washing was washed in public as the media would have used it to the exclusion of anything positive. However, following the 1968 Soviet Intervention in Czechoslovakia, the Party publicly condemned it, and this was followed by increasingly open criticism of the USSR, especially with regard to the arrest of dissidents. The dilemma was attempting a balance that would not merely add to the cold-war rhetoric of the West, but at the same time would let people know of our concerns. Many of us thought that to redress the balance it helped to support the events of the Scotland–USSR Society and its subsidiary Sovscot Tours, and to publicise the positive aspects of the Soviet experiment in the face of a vicious campaign to subvert it in every way. I well remember a remarkable and seminal speech by John Gollan on the problems of the International Communist movement not long before his untimely death. The French Communist Party was much more pro-Soviet, and also very much bigger and more influential than ours. I made contact through a couple of close friends of Gisele who were in the French Party, but they left it over the question of dissent and, as though they had then to justify their action, turned anti-Soviet and dropped out of all political action, convincing Gisele accordingly to look after Number One. From then on I decided not to rock the boat, and my base in France was her family and holidaymaking.

*

As one grows older, uncertainties and problems increase, solutions are less obvious and urgent, whether or not these are personal or political. Of course, the contemplation of uncertainty is uniquely human, not shared by any other species. We have developed a consciousness of ourselves and the world that enables us to ponder the fragility of our existence and that of the lives of others, which, for the majority, is tragic and miserable. A countervailing evolutionary strategy is to allow our hormones to run, to live in the present and enjoy the moment of eating or mating, with the optimism of the struggle to parent our children and the concomitants of working, playing or merely surviving.

An antidote to uncertainty and pessimism lies in religion and superstition and the assumption that science will provide the technical fix that imbues American society. Fortunately younger people everywhere are filled with optimism. Unfortunately, they only learn slowly from history and it is questionable whether human beings will collectively learn quickly enough to cope with the massive problems confronting them.

In the Seventies, I was on the steeper part of a learning curve in both the personal and the political aspects of my life. I was only slowly trying to communicate my feelings, a common failing in the male of the species. I needed an affection that did not cling nor control but, in contrast, I required a certain independence and identity. I needed my own space alongside a close and intimate relationship. I know that Gisele and I were very much in love, and because of that we were a little blind to each other's weaknesses, but it had its high points and has left cherished memories. In addition to Gisele's company and conversation I enjoyed the experiences of new places and faces.

The cultural differences were less important than I had anticipated, but I had not thought sufficiently about how people are motivated and how strong personalities, good in themselves, can also be directed into a power game. I sometimes showed a lack of tact, and I remember once drawing a Venn diagram for Gisele showing how I viewed our different interests. It shocked her to think that I did not anticipate complete overlapping when I thought that two-thirds was a healthy proportion!

More importantly, it seemed to me that Gisele sometimes had a hidden agenda when proposing something that she reasoned was in my best interest, when it actually completely ignored the opinions I had expressed. In other words, she was manipulative and several moves ahead of me.

She realised, too late, that it was self-defeating. Frustrations began to hammer at the door of my patience.

On one occasion I threatened to abandon our holiday in France as she insisted on making all the decisions. Of course, she had the power and the money in France, just as I had it in Britain, but my respect for her wishes weren't reciprocated. At her parents' place at La Saunière I proposed an early return to Aberdeen, and then discovered that my passport and return ticket were missing. Annoyed at this 'blackmailing' I quickly searched and found them in her belongings and immediately drove off. I phoned her from Paris, but she hadn't discovered the truth and giggled with delight at my supposed predicament. I reached Scotland with a different story, as I would have been ashamed to have had to admit that such problems had arisen in my second marriage.

Actually, for some time afterwards we were able to 'kiss and make up'. I was beginning to reassert myself. We agreed to make a fresh start by moving to Aberdeen, to the beautiful Denmore Estate with its ponds, trees and clubhouse. I made a study of its hydrology and ecology, which I used extensively with my students. I also made recommendations, and copies of the booklet were given to all householders, and to Salvesens, the developers, who helped with some of them, such as the ponds.

Following the '74 oil crisis and the exponential increase in house prices, the house we bought in Ellon for three and a half thousand pounds was sold for eleven thousand pounds and we bought 16 Garden Court for sixteen thousand pounds. This was sold for twenty-nine thousand pounds and we paid thirty-five thousand pounds for the luxury apartment at Hyères on the French Riviera, all within the decade of the Seventies.

Five years into our marriage and Gisele's moods changed unpredictably; basically I became disillusioned with the way events were turning out. We attempted, unsuccessfully, a reconciliation through the Aberdeen Marriage Guidance Council. There was one last throw of the dice as Gisele insisted that the real problem was that she was never going to be 'at home' in Britain and that everything would change for the better if we lived in France.

Fortuitously, the college was downsizing, funds were cut and student numbers were limited, especially in the social subjects. Meeting after meeting followed with our union representatives. After long and skilful negotiations, the threatened compulsory redundancies on the basis of 'last in first out', that would have sacked those in their thirties with families and heavy mortgages, were replaced with early retirement and 'Crombie' compensation for the over-fifties.

A condition included a two-year search for an equivalent post in Britain, failing which the compensatory element would be made until the official retiral age had been reached. I was quickly accepted as a supply teacher but I could only earn the difference between my pension and salary of reference before losing the compensatory part. I replaced teachers on sick leave, but couldn't choose the dates to suit the pension conditions, so I took a job designing and selling kitchens from Moben's branch at Dundee, covering all north-east Scotland.

It was American-style one-stop selling on a commission only basis. There were two snags. The hours were unsociable and we had to be 'on call' whether or not there was business. More importantly, Gisele could not accept that I had the two-year commitment to search for an academic post before 'emigrating'.

Despite the circumstances, we moved to France after a year, but I negotiated an arrangement with Moben for periods away to France and I kept a Scottish address. In France I obtained a part-time post as a teacher of English at the PTT College (Post Office & Telephones) a few miles from Hyères.

I wasn't now naive enough to believe that Gisele would suddenly change like a chameleon in a new environment. I thought she would soften up to yet another new start, with all in her favour, and give me the help I needed in settling into a new situation, as I had tried to give her, but there was no reciprocity. Worse! She now exercised her dominance to the full. In my bitter disappointment I took a room in the college hostel for the three week courses and spent the intermediate six weeks selling kitchens in Scotland.

The end of the Seventies was the sad end of my relationship with Gisele and I took out divorce proceedings after thumbing through the local French directory for a solicitor. Gisele was given the right of abode and maintenance until a divorce settlement was reached. This was a poor arrangement for me. My money was locked up in the property and I had no cards to play. Indeed, they were stacked against me as I had not only left my house but I had left the country. She had no incentive to reach an agreement and it took six acrimonious years to conclude, and a mountain of lawyer's bills.

So the decade of the Seventies marked a real change in my lifestyle and thinking. Fortunately, I had my health and my ability to work. I visited my children as often as possible. Sandra and John went from the Ellon Academy to Grays School of Art. Pamela left the University of Edinburgh after one term to marry and have her first child, Tristan, in May 1975, and Verna two years later. She and her family lived in a farmhouse near Lawrencekirk, where Peter replaced a cattleman who had been killed by a kicking bull. I was never sure when I would be able to make another visit so it was always a tremendous pleasure for me to see Pamela and especially Tristan and Verna.

For the first time in my life I felt very uncertain of the future – of the world in general and of myself in particular. I began living day by day. I even toyed with the idea of volunteering to teach English in what remained of Vietnam, after the terrible devastation wreaked by America in its attempt to 'bomb it back to the Stone Age', as General Westmoreland boasted. I thought of other ploys but I was keeping myself occupied selling kitchens and flying to Marseille to take the bi-monthly course in English. So, fortunately, I was earning and saving. Even more fortunately, I met someone else...!

Chapter VIII
The Eighties in Edinburgh

> Those who profess the purity of their
> romanticism, their removal from baser motives
> of self-seeking and pleasure profiteering, are
> often street traders in emotion, barrow-boys of
> the affections – magpies pretending to be
> lovebirds.
>
> William McIlvaney
> *The Kiln*

This someone else was Sadie.   She had been a political
acquaintance since 1963, but had been ring-fenced by me in
that role for the previous seventeen years.   Sadie had
returned to Aberdeen with three small daughters to
continue a university course she had abandoned nearly a
decade earlier, when she met a Sudanese diplomat on a
post-graduate course in Aberdeen, went down to London
with him and then to Khartoum, where they were married.
Following independence from the British, her husband was
posted as district commissioner for the south.   There was a
rebellion against the domination from the Muslim north –
which is still going on, forty years later.   They were
ambushed in their Land Rover, attempting to flee, having
been warned by the police of just such an event.

Her husband was assassinated alongside her, and she was put with a group of survivors and marched across the border to the Belgian Congo, where she managed, after three months trekking through the tropical rainforest, to reach Kenya and the British consulate in Nairobi.

News of her husband's death was quickly communicated back to Britain, but her family, having no news of Sadie, had given her up as dead. She was flown back to Khartoum and joined her husband's family and taught English in a boys' school, an innovation at that time. The Sudanese Government gave her a sizeable compensation for the death of her husband, as he had been following his line of duty. However, she immediately handed it over to her Sudanese relations as they had treated her as one of the family.

A year later she married her deceased husband's brother, who was a medical practitioner, and had three daughters by him, but the marriage failed. This was a Muslim marriage and the only course of action, if she was to retain her children, was to leave the country, which she succeeded in doing after a couple of failed attempts. She landed on her parents' doorstep in the village of Law in Lanarkshire.

Unfortunately her husband gave up his post as a medical practitioner and followed her. He took further qualifications and became a psychiatrist, but eventually Sadie got a separation order, especially as he had refused to pay even the minimum amount of maintenance. This whole saga and sequel warrants a book on its own, but it is not for me to write it.

★

I just called at her door with literature, news sheets and dues stamps for membership of the Communist Party. Being a single parent and teaching full-time, she did well to contribute and take part in activities, but I cannot say that I really knew her. That is, until 1981, when I was selling Moben kitchens and going to France every couple of months to teach a three-week course for English as a foreign language to post office workers on the Riviera. I was staying at the college hostel at La Londe in France and, initially, with daughter Pamela near Lawrencekirk in Scotland. I then rented a flat above a pub in the centre of Stonehaven. I enjoyed every minute of my teaching in France. I wrongly thought that my divorce proceedings were just around the corner and that Gisele and I would soon be going our separate ways.

I was very successful selling kitchens around the whole of the north-east of Scotland and became area manager. Through advertising in national newspapers and periodicals, Moben sent brochures to respondents and then the manager would phone them to obtain appointments for a representative to plan and price a new kitchen, without obligation and free of charge. Moben was founded by a Mr Morris and a Mr Bentham who had sold double glazing on the basis of this one-stop selling technique imported from America. There were three parts to this. The first was planning the kitchen, with the aid of samples, and, in association with the customer's wishes, producing a drawing, discussing finance, installation and confirming at every stage that everything was exactly what the customer wanted, so that it was only the price that was going to be discussed.

We were selling much more than a kitchen. It was a whole array of benefits, desire, envy, power and pride. We then got out our pricing book and calculator and added on a margin in case of errors, or to give a discount – all done before their eyes! We confirmed, yet again, that if the price was right, the plan before them was exactly what they wanted. Then, and only then, did we give them the price and waited in silence. There is an edict that says whoever speaks first is the loser and I must say it was difficult at times not to break the silence myself. Inevitably the reply was 'I'll think about it' which meant they were going to get more quotations, as it was only the price that was under discussion. To close the sale on the night meant giving reasons why it would be possible to give a discount. The skill lay in choosing the most credible and plausible reason out of a possible one hundred and one – and some would actually be true!

We were paid on a commission-only basis, so the pressure was on us, but salespeople who showed this pressure failed to do well. One had to be relaxed and affable. There were occasions when I dug into my commission as further appointments were given to the successful on the basis that 'You are only as good as last night's sale'. The third part of any sale is the documentation and follow-up. Subsequent costs of alterations and necessary additions were invariably allocated to the salesperson and paid out of the commission. Thus the company was always on a winning ticket. The installation teams were also on commission only, so with rented buildings, few salaried staff, low overheads and low capital outlay it was a very profitable company, until many others followed suit and the competition mushroomed and good salespeople became thin on the ground.

I was busy. I was doing well, but my personal life was at a low ebb and I felt the loneliness of a long-distance runner.

As I was returning from an aborted sales pitch down Clifton Road, Aberdeen, one evening, I stopped and rang Sadie's front doorbell. After almost losing contact, we reminisced over a cup of coffee. I realised that she was most welcoming and we made a date at a restaurant. The conversation ranged far wider than the old times of demonstrations, meetings, policies and personalities. She invited me back to her flat, and told me some time later that she was surprised that I didn't stay overnight.

Actually I was surprised that we were getting on so well, and I wasn't going to jeopardise this new-found relationship by precipitate or impulsive action. However, it wasn't long before I moved in, and even if the world had stopped at that moment, I would have always been eternally grateful for the warmth, understanding and affection which turned me round completely out of a state of confusion. The timing was perfect, and weeks, months and years of a happy relationship followed.

In 1982 I won the company prize of a Caribbean holiday and took Sadie to Cuba. We went walking over the Yorkshire Dales, to Leningrad for a winter festival of opera and ballet, to China, France, the Soviet Union, including Tashkent, Samarkand and Buhkara. On a later occasion, her son-in-law's wealthy parents accompanied us to Armenia, Azerbajan and Georgia. Sadie and I also went sailing in Turkey and around the Greek Islands.

During term-time we took trips down to Lanarkshire to see her parents, and to Edinburgh and her three daughters. We were both exceedingly occupied within our own space, and no one is more independently minded than Sadie, but when we had time together it was a rich and rewarding experience. In contrast to my life in the Seventies, there was no power struggle and manipulation. I may have read

Sadie's mind wrongly at times, but I followed her decision to retire early and move to Edinburgh to separate flats.

She bought a large but neglected one and completely renovated it to her own specifications. It included an office that would be used to organise a school to teach English as a foreign language, with me as principal and herself as director of studies. We had a brilliant brochure printed for 'Anglospeak', and I taught a summer course at the Edinburgh Tutorial College in preparation. We advertised and obtained some individuals from Spain, Italy and France, and the following summer went on a package holiday to Yugoslavia where her cousin introduced us to an agency in Belgrade. Unfortunately, the arrangements were cancelled at short notice as they had insufficient applications and only one turned up.

I have quite vivid memories of a holiday with Sadie in the Croatian coastal area of Yugoslavia. The local Croatians working there grumbled that the hard currency earned by the tourist trade went to Serbia, when I thought that Yugoslavia was then a very friendly and united country and it never occurred to me that the Croatians would go to war for their independence!

One evening, Sadie and I were sitting at one of the long tables in the 'beer garden' of the hotel and a group of a dozen men about my age came in speaking German. I said, jokingly, to Sadie, 'Here comes a U-boat crew'. They sat down on the empty benches opposite us and, yes indeed, they were German navy veterans on a 'club holiday'. For the first time, I shook hands with an ex-U-boat officer, suppressing my natural emotions. To this day I associate the German language with my images of the war, but I hope that I am able to rationalise the situation and act accordingly, but at the same time understand how some people's behaviour is controlled by their emotions and not their intellect.

My stable relationship with Sadie, together with regular but part-time teaching, resulted in a renewal of my political work, and also more regular contact with my extending family.

Pamela's marriage broke up and she went to live with Hans Bracker, who originally came from West Germany. Instead of conscription into the army he did community gardening work, and through the Rudolph Steiner network he was subsequently employed as a gardener at Templehill in Kincardineshire, where he involved the mentally handicapped inmates in assisting him.

Pam and Hans lived in a small cottage near Auchenblae where two more children were born, Catriona in 1982 and Jan in 1985. They were very overcrowded, but not long after, an old Victorian house in the centre of Auchenblae came on the market. Its former use was as the registry office and it needed complete renovation. With the financial help of myself and Hans's father in Germany, they bought it, and Hans undertook the immense task of changing it from a shell to a fine family house. This took a period of years so that each time I visited them it had the air of a building site, but with high quality additions and alterations so it allowed the six of them to have a reasonable standard of living.

Auntie Marge, my father's sister, was now ninety, and the only one left of that generation, so I organised a grand reunion of the Newtons in Lancashire, as illustrated by the photograph in the car park of the hotel. It was a singularly memorable event as we were never a close family and were spread out all over Britain and around the globe. We had always maintained contact, but the break-up of our

Top: Peace Festival retirement party, Assembly Rooms, Edinburgh, October, 1993.
Bottom: The Peace Festival Committee at work in the Friends Meeting House, 1992.

Top: Patrolling Faslane submarine base on the peace boat *Puffin,* 1993.
Bottom: With Tristan on our first boat near Faslane.

Top: You know Pat, we should enjoy here while we're here, 'cos there's no here there.
Bottom: Tristan and 'Scottish weather' in the Caribbean, 1997. (see page 200.)

Top: Hello MI5, I'd like to know whether you've got a file on me, and if not,why not?
Bottom: Success, at last, in the struggle for a participatory type of democracy in Scotland.

marriages seemed to mirror the national statistics. Perhaps arranged marriages have something to be said for them after all!

In sum, my personal problems, uncertainties and the catharsis of the Seventies were transformed into a contented stability and I was at ease with myself. The political scene was being transformed in the opposite direction in a newly found muddle of change, but I was now able to return to an active role instead of being merely an interested observer.

Not long after we moved to Edinburgh in 1984, Sadie and I offered our help to the Miners' Welfare in Dalkeith during the famous Miners' Strike. We took food and jumble and met some outstanding characters in both the miners and their wives. There was a great feeling of camaraderie and solidarity, and support groups in Edinburgh were continually growing throughout the twelve months of the strike. I thought that Mick McGahey would have handled the strike better than Arthur Scargill by a more subtle campaign against government policy, balloting members and forcing negotiations to acceptable solutions, but I have no doubt whatever about the sheer ruthlessness of the Thatcher Government in its diabolical objectives.

Few people realised at the time that the Thatcher Government had planned for it during the previous years by building up stocks of coal, changing the power stations' fuel to oil, building gas-fired and nuclear-powered stations, bringing in laws restricting the activities of trades unions and stopping social security payments to the families of striking miners. The Government, in its aim to make the trades unions ineffective, knew that it had to defeat the miners 'no matter the cost', and spent one billion pounds in doing so.

Part of the attack was the involvement of the secret services, detailed in the hundreds of pages of Seumas Milne's 1994 book, *The Enemy Within*, stating that no effort nor expense was spared, 'from the secret financing of strike-breakers to mass electronic surveillance, from the manipulation of agents provocateurs to attempts to "fit-up" miners' officials, in order to discredit the union and its leaders. It is a record of the abuse of unaccountable power...' etc. Miners' wives, who had previously been passive observers, became active on their husbands' behalf. Many of them became politically literate and remarkably eloquent and I knew some of them who subsequently took education courses and interesting jobs, so that the legacy of the strike was not altogether negative.

*

At about the same time I joined the local CND group in Stockbridge, which met in the primary school the first Monday evening of every month. It was a very flourishing campaigning group of two hundred with about forty active members. I joined a rota at the stall in the centre of Stockbridge every Saturday morning, selling badges and books, but also giving away leaflets and our current newsletter, as well as asking people to sign a petition or, indeed, to join us. Local and national demonstrations were well supported and our vertical banners made by Dick Sneddon became well known for their distinctiveness, as on the photo, in which I am pictured with my back to the camera! In December our own Christmas card was distributed, inviting people to our carol singing under the council-erected illuminated tree, but my own interest lay in the problem of how to influence our decision-makers. I became the group's representative on the council's newly formed Peace Forum.

In 1984 Thatcher was riding high as a consequence of the jingoism of the Falklands War, but in Edinburgh the long-standing Conservative majority was overturned by Labour. In 1985, the convenor of the Peace Forum, Councillor Dickie Alexander, proposed a Peace Weekend in the Assembly Rooms, George Street, for the beginning of March 1986. These prestigious premises belonged to the council and were administered by their recreation department. They included different-sized rooms and halls and were readily available at this slack time of the year.

I proposed that it should be a Peace Festival with a whole range of events for a wide variety of organisations, involving as many people as possible, with serious meetings, light entertainment, exhibitions and stalls, and a café and a bar all under the one roof. A small organising committee was formed, including myself, Alan Wilkie and John Doney from the Peace Forum, Roger Jones, deputy director of the recreation department, the manager of the Assembly Rooms and Councillor Alexander, with myself as the main co-ordinator. Its outstanding success led to an independent committee being elected, chaired by myself, with a grant from the council to organise a second one in 1987, which was almost too ambitious for the volunteers, who were experiencing this for the first time but, again, it was outstandingly successful, whatever criteria could be applied.

At first, there were fruitless discussions about who to exclude and sectarian rivalries emerged, but these soon gave way in practice to exciting co-operative ventures where it became obvious that we were all ploughing the same furrow. But what was the motivating force behind my

initiatives?   Memoirs are written with the benefit of
hindsight and, all too often, a 'spin' is put on what was
thought to have been said and acted upon. The brutal truth
is probably only in the history recorded at the time, so the
best answer might be in this extract from a speech I made
to local government employees at a conference in Japan in
October 1992, when I was invited to the International
Conference of Nuclear-Free Zone Authorities.   After a
general introduction I said:

> All cities have two faces – a shiny top and a
> shadowy bottom, and Edinburgh is no
> exception. The other side of our city of half a
> million shows a widening gap between the rich
> and the poor, increasing drugs and Aids
> problems, rising crime and unemployment,
> and chronic congestion from more and more
> private cars.
>
> The professional classes are also ill at ease
> with the situation. Many of them now vote
> Labour so that, for the first time in
> Edinburgh's history, the Labour Party gained
> control of the city's administration in 1984.
> Very often, a change in the political
> complexion of a council results in little change
> for the average citizen, as there is a lot of
> inertia to overcome. In any case, the British
> Government in London, through its Scottish
> secretary of state, has increased its control,
> especially financially, in the council's affairs.
>
> The new Labour Council of Edinburgh
> decided to publicise its efforts with a slogan,
> 'Improving Services, Creating Jobs'.   They

distributed broadsheets of information, opened up the City Chambers to local organisations, encouraged the setting up of community councils, and formed advisory committees with representatives of local organisations.

These measures have helped to remove some of the alienation of the population from the decision-making process. Access and accountability with freedom of information is sadly lacking in our so-called democracy, so I rated these changes as being significant, even though they did not make headline news. The present representative type of democracy is inadequate because it tends to encourage a paternalistic attitude by councillors, as they can make decisions with little need to consult. Pressures from existing vested interests often leads to an acceptance of the 'Establishment' view. Thus, the *status quo* is preserved. When change is needed in favour of those without the influence and power of property and money, a more radical type of democracy is required.

Let me give you an example by showing how we have linked the peace movement with the council. Conservative and other politicians declare that issues of peace and security are the prerogative of central government and outside the remit of the local. However, during the Cold War, local authorities were obliged to organise systems of civil defence, build deep bomb-proof bunkers for officials and distribute information to all citizens in case of nuclear war with the USSR. Every householder was asked to store tins of beans and water under the stairs in case of emergency. People were shown how to whitewash their windows to prevent incoming radiation and to stay in their houses until told by radio to do otherwise.

You, who are well aware of the consequences of even small, unsophisticated atomic bombs, may well laugh at such ridiculous instructions, but they were meant to get the population used to the idea that nuclear war was not only inevitable, but winnable.

The peace organisations, together with the trades unions and labour movement, challenged the authorities on the details of such a policy. The Edinburgh Council proclaimed its intention to become a nuclear-free zone and turned its Emergency Planning Committee into an Advisory Committee on Peace Matters as a sub-committee of the Council. Thus, the policy of civil defence was exposed as a dishonest campaign, imposed on the local authority against its will.

For forty years my main interest has been the Campaign for Nuclear Disarmament. Even though the Cold War and the nonsense of civil defence are things of the past, today Britain's first of four giant Trident submarines is coming to Scotland, to be armed with a new generation of nuclear weapons, multiplying our nuclear capacity eightfold, at a time when the USA and Russia are decreasing theirs. Our reason is, of course, nothing to do with defence. It has never been the case. It stems from our imperial past and our rulers' 'Great Power' chauvinism, maintaining our permanent seat in the UN Security Council and other international bodies.

So the essential element is the linkage of national to local concerns, and to involve more people and their organisations in the decision-making process. I thus represented CND on the Advisory Committee and initiated the Edinburgh Peace Festival. An independent committee of organisations was formed, receiving financial assistance from the council. So what are its aims?

Firstly, it aims to bring together those who want to build a civil society based on social justice, the peaceful settlement of disputes, religious and ethnic understanding, ecological responsibility and nuclear disarmament.

Secondly, it provides events ranging from concerts to conferences, from displays to discussions, from exhibitions to entertainment, with national and international performers and speakers.

Thirdly, it promotes the theme 'Think Globally, Act Locally', involving all sections of the community, linking individuals, grassroots organisations and decision-making bodies, advancing and not detracting from the identity of each.

I then explained to my audience that a mere representative type of democracy can lead to an elected dictatorship, the need for a more participatory type, and the adoption of a more pragmatic approach when the complexities of human behaviour are appreciated but not made the excuse for delaying action for the empowerment of individuals and their organisations.

I concluded, then, by saying that: 'The end result is that by empowering more people, the whole of society benefits. Ordinary citizens will see the need to solve all problems by peaceful negotiation and are made familiar with the machinery necessary to achieve this. It has always seemed important to me that democratic centralism should not only be 'top down' but also 'bottom up', and that means a lot of hard work at grass-roots level.'

*

One of the proudest moments of my life was the presentation by the City of Edinburgh of the Sir William Y. Darling Award for Good Citizen of the Year 1988 in recognition of my work in the peace movement. I claimed at the time that this award reflected more honour on the Council than on me, for its recognition of the value of a strong peace movement in Edinburgh with which I was proud to be associated. I gave the money to the Peace Festival and I recall that Sir William Y. Darling had been a well-known Tory holding high office in a former administration not noted for his sympathies with any of the organisations with which I was associated. His grandson, Alistair Darling, MP for Edinburgh Central and presently Chief Secretary to the Treasury in the Blair Government, told me, with his tongue in cheek, that his grandfather would be turning in his grave if he had known that I had been a recipient of such an award!

In order to fill in what I thought were gaps in the thinking of leading contributors to an international meeting on peace and security held over several days in Berlin in the GDR, June 1988, this is what I said as the delegate from the Scottish Committee of the Communist Party.

> I'd like to focus your attention on a different approach to 'development'. The key point is this. Human activity is now a major ecological factor – not yet fully appreciated, but well understood. The scale, acceleration and direction of growth and development are going to threaten rather than help the well-being of humanity as we move into the next century. Therefore, development must be shown to be sustainable.
>
> After several thousand generations of *Homo sapiens*, in my one lifetime world population has tripled. More importantly, urbanisation, industrialisation, soil erosion, pollution, depletion of non-renewable resources and the number of people living in poverty have increased manyfold.

I then developed the theme of development and the seductive power of consumerism, attacking the 'more of everything' sloganeering of some of the participants.

The UN Bruntland Report, 'Our Common Future', had just been published, and in conversation it was obviously not in the hands of the very people who were in a position to make decisions, including a minister from one of the African nations. Of course, in subsequent years, ever-increasing publicity and concern led to limited action by governments, but the Eastern bloc was as guilty as any in their views on sustainable development, and even now the concept is largely misunderstood.

I designed an exhibition and a questionnaire on the environment and the Bruntland report and made a survey of opinion assisted by Lynne Devine, presenting a report to the Peace Forum which was then published. Since then, of course, the problems have been widely discussed in the media and 'green' movements have expanded.

★

I have been privileged with a number of informal meetings with comrades from the Soviet Union and especially with a delegation in 1987. I remember discussions with the Moscow police inspectors and asking how the police on duty are prevented from abusing their powers. In particular, we had an excellent exchange of views with members of the central committee of the Kiev Communist Party, for example, on the tendency for any bureaucracy to look first to its own interests before those they purported to serve, of the need to institutionalise checks and balances on those holding political power and for access to information which governments otherwise wrongly withhold in the name of 'national security' in order to avoid valid criticism.

As an aside, I must say that I am often astonished that writers are supposedly able to quote verbatim from conversations held years previously – how he said one thing, and she replied another, ad infinitum! I suspect that it is all invented for effect because readers generally like a conversational style. I haven't followed this tradition until this example, which wasn't recorded, but was along the lines of what is set out below.

Announcing that I came from Scotland where there was
much discussion of the problems of nationalism and
democracy, the conversation continued roughly as follows:

RAY: Why do Jews in the USSR have to state that
fact on their passports?

1ST SEC: In the USSR there are many nationalities and
this is stated on their passports.

RAY: Is not Judaism a religion and not a
nationality?

1ST SEC: The Jews don't see it that way, especially the
Zionists whose allegiance is first to the Jewish
state of Israel and only second to the USSR.

RAY: Is your allegiance first to the Ukraine and
secondly to the USSR?

1ST SEC: Probably increasingly so. (Smiles all round)

RAY: So are the many Russians in the Ukraine
second class citizens?

1ST SEC: Of course not. They are our valuable
partners.

RAY: But I detect a difference in attitude to
Russians and Jews, but let me ask a further
question. Is there not a problem with
Moscow as the capital of Russia and also of
the USSR?

1ST SEC: Why should there be? I don't understand.

RAY: Because it seems to many of us in Scotland
that because London is the capital of England
and also the capital of the United Kingdom

they confuse Britishness, Englishness and Scottishness, and have inherited unconsciously the imperialist notion of imposing on us policies against our will. All federal states have found serious problems when the capital of the union wasn't a separate entity such as Washington, Ottawa and Canberra. Many people, I suspect, in your republics, see Moscow as a Russian capital imposing a Russian will. Now supposing Leningrad had been made the capital of the union, separate from Moscow as capital of Russia...

CHAIRMAN: We don't see it that way as the republics are autonomous. Next question please.

Other members of the delegation asked questions on the role of women, the advantages of having a self-employed sector, problems of food production and distribution, and the separation of the Party from the State machine. Feedback from the interpreter the next day revealed that when we had gone there was a heated discussion on our comments; he mentioned that it was the first time after many years of interpreting that he had heard so many challenging remarks. I mention this because they gave as the excuse for a closed society the understandable security problem – their defence against the West was secrecy as well as arms. On the other hand, it enables those in power not to be challenged by the very real problems as they emerge, so that a kind of stagnation results and society loses out.

Being on the sidelines meant that I was without influence, but I also know that the CPGB only slowly learnt of the excesses of oppression in the Soviet Union and China as they were revealed much later from authoritative sources rather than from 'enemy propaganda'. Nevertheless, the international department of the Party made its views known in private conversations and, in general, were welcome for what diplomats call 'frank and full discussions'. At the end of the day, however, the tail can't wag the dog.

One question remains. After the collapse of the Soviet Union and many of the communist parties, was my participation a wasted effort? I think not.

The archives will show that the activities of the British Communist Party were overwhelmingly concerned with national and local problems that other British parties did not seem to be tackling with sufficient knowledge, understanding, commitment and vigour.

The Communist Party of Great Britain, in contrast to the CPSU, was no place for anyone wanting a career in politics. Those people, and I have known many, went to the Labour Party and I don't blame them. Indeed I respect their attempts to get to where power lies, but some were merely opportunists and integrity often went out of the window. I could name names but that would not get us anywhere.

I have benefited personally from the company of comrades whose devotion to the various struggles was exemplary and it showed in their attitudes to their fellow human beings. In other words it rubbed off and gave one a unique sense of purpose and a positive attitude to life in general. But inevitably the Communist Party was internationalist in outlook – we are our brother's keeper as there is only one human kind. We have the common problem of the rich in all countries getting together to devise policies that exploit the poor. International solidarity was therefore required of us, and the Soviet Union had the only game in town, so we had to play the same tune. The questions and doubts many had were a luxury, or so it seemed at the time, when the threat of nuclear annihilation was very real. For example, I found no difficulty in accepting both the unilateral approach of CND and the multilateral policy of the CPGB. For me, the priority was the same: to influence public opinion and galvanise people into action to stop the Government from fanning the flames of the nuclear arms race and to redeploy those resources for social use.

Now the archives in Moscow are revealing how near to collapse the Soviet system has been since its inception in 1917, and books are now being written from both sides of the equation – emphasising either the role of the key players like Lenin and Stalin or the circumstances which did not allow any other policies to be implemented.

It seems to me that history confirms Marx's prerequisites for socialism being built out of the most advanced capitalist countries and not the most backward as in Russia. Also the 'domino effect' of world revolution did not take place.

Indeed, counter-revolution and the suppression of communist parties everywhere have been the name of the game ever since 1917. The wars of intervention, civil strife, famine and economic collapse forced Lenin and then Stalin into extreme measures, initially to enable the socialist revolution to survive by progressively banning all opposition, and then by 'liquidating' even communists who were said by someone to be a 'dissident', so that an oppressive one-party state was built up. Oscar Lange, one of the socialist planners, said on his death bed, 'I would have been a Bukharinite gradualist (executed by Stalin before the war), yet as I think back, I ask myself, again and again, was there an alternative to the indiscriminate, brutal, basically unplanned rush forward of the first Five-Year Plan? I wish I could say there was, but I cannot. I cannot find an answer.'

For instance, would the corrupt and incompetent Russia of the Romanovs, 'our allies in World War I', have built such an advanced industrial and literate state out of the ruins of a backward and peasant-based economy? Instead we can be grateful for its existence during World War II. As Eric Hobsbawm eloquently and authoritatively wrote in his seminal work *The Age of Extremes*, 'Only the temporary and bizarre alliance of liberal capitalism and communism in self-defence against world fascism saved democracy, for the victory over Hitler's Germany was essentially won, and could only have been won, by the Red Army.' Then in the post-war years the United States raised the stakes so high in the arms race that the USSR bankrupted itself and capitalism took over.

I therefore view the world scene, like an individual human being, as one of great complexity and full of game plans and contradictions. Like the Miners' Strike of '84, the Soviet Union, in my opinion, was not going to be allowed to succeed WHATEVER THE COST. This, however, can be a reason for resistance and not submission, as in present-day Cuba, in what was formerly a key issue, the class struggle.

Chapter IX
The Nineties in Retirement

> 'We are going to a different world,' said
> Candide, 'and I expect it is the one where all
> goes well; for I must admit that regrettable
> things happen in this world of ours, moral and
> physical acts that one cannot approve of.'
>
> Voltaire
> *Candide*

By 1994 Sadie and I were drifting apart, hearing the other's
answers before the same questions were again posed. My
respect, gratitude and happy memories of our years
together had not decreased, but it seemed to me that Sadie
was jealously guarding her independent living, thinking and
working to the extent that I would have to be content with
a weekend friendship and only a partial relationship or
none at all. Ambiguity crept in. When is a friendship
destroyed by the ending of a sexual relationship? Do I want
to spend my 'sunset' years just doing my own thing?
Women now have more freedom to choose and this is also
good for men, but there must be reciprocity. We had come
to a decision.

In October I collected my dressing gown that was
hanging unused behind her bedroom door and removed

my bedroom slippers from the hall cupboard. We were now like friendly neighbours, exchanging the latest oddments of news and occasionally reminiscing, especially on the political past. The main topic was her grandchildren. She was always extremely concerned about their welfare and it was delightful to accompany her with the pram to the Botanic Gardens or the 'Scotland Yard' swing park.

For the rest of the year I dropped in for coffee and a Kit Kat, but she was unable to return the call. I counted my blessings, and there were many, but then wondered about the rest of my retirement and whether there was anybody out there in the big wide world of single women looking for male companionship. But how do people make contact? The personal ads seemed a bit corny and an odd way of starting a friendship let alone a relationship. Anyway, these must be strange individuals seeking an answer to their own inadequacies. In any case, I'm carrying, like everybody else of my age, a lot of baggage from my professional, political, family and personal life that I just can't jettison.

In the *New Statesman* was an advert by 'Socialist Partners', half-price for the over-sixties, so I sent away. This was all new to me, but intriguing. I filled in the questionnaire and, in return, received copies of others that the organisation had deemed a likely match and which gave first names and telephone numbers. I cut my teeth (not literally!) on several encounters, following the advice given to meet for coffee or drink in a 'neutral' rendezvous and then on to restaurants, the theatre and home visits. Some were mutually ended at the first encounter. Others went slightly longer, but having exhausted the lists I advertised locally and received about twenty replies. I treated them at first like job applications, made a short list, interviewed them and Pat got the job!

No, it wasn't quite like that. From the profiles it was easy to reject. The rest I phoned and some conversations added substantially to my phone bill. I found that it was subsequently easy to meet and to say goodbye or to arrange a further meeting. It was interesting but also frustrating. I was prepared to take risks, but not to start a relationship that had no potential for the future.

I was already seeing others when I met Pat for the first time in Hamilton's Bar in Stockbridge at 9 p.m. on January 24th, 1995. There was an immediate meeting of minds. The next time involved a walk from Carlops into the snow-covered Pentlands followed by a pub lunch. We held hands and embraced.

I cancelled other rendezvous. An evening meal at my place evolved into a weekend at hers, with an intermingling of minds and limbs that young people only read and dream about. From the start there were no hidden agendas, no glass walls to shatter, no doubts, but also no illusions. I told Sadie, who knew from the outset about my 'marketing' arrangements, which she treated with great amusement until that moment of truth.

★

At heart I'm a serial monogamist, and a new beginning means turning the page. This involves negative as well as decidedly positive aspects. Making a clean break with someone you've shared part of your life with is a momentous occasion. What isn't always realised is that it also results in cutting off the contacts with her family and friends as a necessary commitment to one's new partner.

Of course, the man then makes new friends and contacts, and these new associations are very rarely highlighted. We may not be marrying into an extended family and property – the norm for the aristocracy – but we enter a new arena of friends and social events that can be restricting or liberating.

Pat and I were in love and nobody was more surprised than ourselves. This was no teenage head-over-heels fantasy. We both had our feet on the ground and realised the potential, gradually accommodating our external commitments and enforced absence into an inexorable coupling of lives and lifestyles. Even now I would caution anyone reciting the same kind of story that they are probably infatuated, deluded, immature or worse!

After surviving so many years on this planet, a lot of water has gone under the bridge, bringing doubts if not cynicism. Attempts at playing the devil's advocate failed. The uncanny harmony of both intention and action led to an unsurpassed quality of life and a self-fulfilment that can only be expressed in poetry and music – but all relationships change. Our task was to make it change into the direction we both desired.

I had retired as co-ordinator of the Edinburgh Peace Festival in October 1993, after a memorable social evening and presentation at the Assembly Rooms. However, I continued to assist with certain events, especially the civic forum in the New Parliament Building in 1995, and the Campaign for Scottish Democracy. The election of a Labour Government on the 1st May 1997 reflected a sea change in the mood of the British people for a more caring and sharing society. I doubt whether there will, in fact, be much of a shift in that direction as there has been no real challenge to the Thatcherite policies that preceded it. In Scotland, however, the Tories were left with no MP's, no

MEP's and no control of any council. They then fought a losing battle in the referendum for Scotland's Parliament with vitriolic publicity on the costs involved showing yet again that they know the price of everything but the value of nothing. One of my letters to the *Scotsman* included the following:

> If Conservative supporters of the 'No' campaign really believe that the status quo in Scotland is the best of all possible worlds, then they should campaign for the elimination of Westminster and accept governance from Brussels via a Secretary of State of the UK. It would be much cheaper than the present arrangement but surely not as democratic? I forget, of course, that the word *democracy* never passes the lips of the 'No' campaigners.

Ironically, the only hope the Tories have got in order to get a foot in the Scottish door is in the proposed Parliament with proportional representation. I wholeheartedly agree that they should be so represented, and with the more consensual and participatory type of democracy envisaged all voices need to be heard.

★

I see in my diary a sprinkling of visits by Pat's friends, often to an evening meal, a few theatre bookings and then, on April 1st, 1995, moving to Pat's and getting my own flat ready for letting. We had a week's holiday in common at Easter and went to the Greek Ionian Islands on a sailing holiday with a Sunsail flotilla. This was quite a new venture for Pat. It was obviously going to decide whether we would be sailing together in the future.

She must have had more than a little affection for me to have taken such a courageous step as she admitted her phobia about water, but she quickly adapted to the completely new challenge. This was subsequently followed by day sails in 'Eala Bheag' from Port Edgar and a week's exciting family 'reunion' on the forty-four foot luxury yacht, *Magic Flute*, from Croahb Haven to Tobermory, Barra and Iona.

But what of my own motivation, experience and qualifications in seafaring and for how long had I been sailing small boats as opposed to the ships of my youth?

The origins go back to my primary school days, exploring the beaches at Birkdale and Southport, seeing the ships on the horizon as well as the permanent profiles of wrecks between the low and high water marks. The marine environment was therefore imprinted on my memory so that when I went to the Outward Bound course in Aberdovey at the age of sixteen, it was like taking a duckling to water. The background and interest was there and it was a matter of gaining the necessary knowledge, skills and experience. This was, in fact, my first sailing experience with small boats, followed by the schooner, *Prince Louis*, which had been loaned by

Gordonstoun School of Kurt Hahn, on whose philosophy the Outward Bound School was based.

Actually, this was the last time I sailed until I retired nearly fifty years later! In the late Eighties Sadie and I joined as paying crew of a forty-five foot Gaff-rigged boat, *Peace Messenger*, in one of the legs of the voyage round the Irish Sea in a CND project, calling attention to the problems, for instance, of fishing boats being dragged under by submarines and of nuclear leaks from Sellafield. We visited Dundalk, Dublin, Cork and Fishguard with civic and Irish CND receptions and meetings especially those organised by Adi Roche, who was to become an Irish presidential candidate.

Peace Messenger was a heavy boat of wooden construction, but eminently seaworthy. Nevertheless, she couldn't sail too close to the wind and leaving Cork we had problems with the engine, but it was great being under sail. It brought home the need to work with nature, and not against it, with a continuous weather eye on the alert for changes which could take place quite suddenly.

A boat has got to be self-sufficient in all things, with the ultimate in space planning. The crew, too, must be self-reliant, working together as a team, not because a rule book says so, but because it is obvious to all the crew for the smooth running and safety of the boat. Neither can anyone escape! The art of living together in a confined space, the challenge of getting there in terms of good seamanship and navigation, and the satisfaction of a job well done made me thirsty for more. The sea is no respecter of persons. It forces all members of the crew to look at the objectives rather than at the idiosyncrasies of each other. Those on an ego trip soon find themselves looking for another boat or an alternative activity.

Fortuitously, I then met Iain Nicholls when we were visiting the Faslane Peace Camp. He was looking for crew to sail his twenty-eight foot Gaffer, *Puffin*, to Iona and, if possible, to Northern Ireland, where he had contacts involved in reconciliation. A hundred year old boat needs a lot of looking after, like an aged aunt. We had problems, including an engine fault, so we never reached our destination, but got as far as Tobermory. It was too risky to continue further without auxiliary power, so we returned under sail only, round the Mull of Kintyre, including a wonderful overnight sail under a canopy of stars and moonlight, with a following wind taking *Puffin* back to its mooring in the Gareloch near Rhu.

I made a number of smaller trips with Iain in *Puffin*, but it was very demanding in terms of time and energy, and Iain did not have the kind of money needed to bring it up to a really good and reliable standard, despite the injection of cash from the Peace Project funds of Christian CND. Iain spent most of his time throughout the year maintaining and servicing, making do and mending, and managed to 'show the flag' – a large CND symbol on the mainsail – at Faslane and the Lower Clyde for some years.

I was now becoming involved in the art of yachting, but when I inquired about chartering one they demanded evidence of qualifications, as well as relevant experience, so I enrolled at an evening class at the Jewel and Esk College, formerly Leith Nautical College. I obtained my RYA Coastal Skipper's Shorebased and also Practical Certificates and the following year the Ocean Skipper's, so now I was well kitted out to hire any boat I wanted.

By this time, my grandson, Tristan, had been introduced to sailing via the Ocean Youth Training scheme, and had joined my two brothers and myself on a hired yacht on

Loch Ness and the Great Glen. This had been a last minute change from sailing off the coast of Yugoslavia which we had planned months earlier before hostilities finally broke out.

Iain had heard about a reconstructed hull of a nineteen foot wooden boat in a joiner's shed in Dumbarton, and Tristan and I bought it for one thousand, nine hundred pounds, little realising the enormous amount of work and expense it would take to fit it out ready for sea. We called it *Calaman*, Gaelic for dove or pigeon, and used it for a season day-sailing from its mooring near Rhu. It was time-consuming driving from Edinburgh, rowing out and preparing it for a sail. It had a very good specification, including twin-burner stove and VHF radio, but the cabin was too small to contemplate overnight stays and we sold it to recoup our investment and to look for a better one.

This was to be a superb specimen of a Folkboat type of yacht, *Kuruwa*, bought from the chief coastguard at Gourock. Strange to say, Roger Clarke had been the navigator on the *Peace Messenger*, and immediately there was a fine rapport which helped Tristan a lot in the management of the boat. *Kuruwa* had been professionally refurbished in Skye and had excellent design qualities.

Tristan sailed it frequently while he was at the Glasgow Nautical College on a marine engineering course, but then took a job with Mobil Oil Tankers. As the prospect was only an occasional sail and I had access to a boat in Edinburgh, that too was sold and our investment again recovered.

In the summer of 1996, Tristan was looking for a change from the continuous months at sea, followed by a long, but unoccupied leave when his friends were either working or studying. He therefore left Mobil Tankers and joined an

Aberdeen tug company. His social life could now be more easily planned and he was also in a position to go sailing again. The search for a boat with good headroom which was fit for offshore sailing accelerated. It occurred to me that he was keen to move up but didn't have the funds to do this properly and get what he really wanted.

I therefore joined with him in the purchase of a 1970 Rival 31. It was very well equipped as well as offering many possibilities, berthing four in comfort to any part of the globe. *Rival Lady* was owned by a Bob Jamieson, who was hoping to sail the Atlantic until ill health had forced him to abandon the project. Funnily enough, I had met Bob three years previously when we were taking our Ocean Skipper's course, and I had sold him our mooring in the Gareloch for the boat he had just then acquired – *Rival Lady*! We had it surveyed, bought it and had it transported to Peterhead Marina at the beginning of 1997.

I was also very happy to sail with Mike and Margaret MacGregor in their twenty-three foot Elizabethan GRP and Bermudan rigged boat, *Eala Bheag*. I had known Margaret's parents in Aberdeen as they had been good CP members. Her father, Bill Morrice, had done a great deal of good work in the Aberdeen Trades Council Club, and I had known Margaret vaguely when she was a student. Many years later I met her campaigning as a Labour candidate in the council elections in which she was successful, eventually convening committees, giving up her job in primary teaching and then becoming deputy Lord Provost.

Mike was keen, but was only a recently experienced sailor, and we sailed frequently on the Forth, with or without our partners and friends from its berth at the Port Edgar Marina to and from Charleston, Brucehaven, Inchcolm, Blackness, Grangemouth, Aberdour, Cramond and Granton, usually stopping off at the Two Bridges Hotel in South Queensferry for a pie and a pint on the way back.

Those who know these places realise that they are tidal. In other words they can be entered only two or three hours on either side of high tide, so the timing had to be exact. It also mattered whether the Forth was ebbing or flooding as it could run at over a knot, so that sailing through the water at four knots could be either three or five knots over the ground. The wind direction and speed varies in the Firth, even from the general weather forecast, owing to the configuration of the land, and I was surprised at the variety of conditions that had to be catered for within a relatively small area.

There is no doubt that the west coast of Scotland is one of the best sailing areas in Europe, but having the facility of taking a boat out only half an hour after leaving home enables one to take advantage at a moment's notice of appropriate weather conditions at a time of one's choosing, so Pat and I have often just taken the boat out for a pleasant and enjoyable hour.

Thus, enjoying life together in this multifaceted way, we 'grew' together and our relationship matured. A pattern began to reveal itself: visits by her daughter, Shona, by friends such as Connie and Bill from Bath, Sheila from Toronto, Kirsty from Vancouver, and from my own family, especially Pamela, Tristan, Catriona and Jan. Many weekend evenings were spent playing bridge with her elderly 'aunt', Muriel, who was keen to teach the game to Pat.

I had learnt to play bridge in France with Gisele's sister and brother-in-law, but played only spasmodically. I did not wish to join a bridge club as Sadie didn't want to learn, so I was pleased, at last, to engage in friendly sessions with

Muriel, Rita and Pat, interrupted by a glass of sherry and then coffee and sandwiches. Previously, I had gained the impression from others that bridge parties tended to be rather pretentious affairs, cultivating a serious post-mortem of every move with creative tensions within the group. However, these occasional evenings acted as an escape and a change from the serious so they were relaxing as well as challenging.

Bridge to me seems to reflect, to a limited extent, the struggle of life itself; competition but also co-operation with one's partner, the luck of the draw (we are dealt with a set of one hundred thousand genes as a set of thirteen cards), but with a heavy emphasis on the skill necessary to play the hand you are given in the circumstances provided by the other players. Indeed, in board bridge the same hands are played by moving round the tables, so that everybody should get the same number of points, but they don't! Those using the opportunities to the best of their advantage win, as in real life, except that in the real world we don't start from zero. A few have a lot of points given to them before they start competing, whereas many have the cards stacked against them from the start and are kept in that subservient situation. The fact that only a few are chosen to be moved up the ladder (e.g. assisted places at public schools) gives a false impression of equal opportunity. Like all the analogies the comparison of bridge and the art of living is simplistic, but I think this is the reason why it is probably the most enjoyable card game yet invented.

★

Pat and I had hopefully learnt from our previous relationships, as well as from the fact that growing older forces one to think more deeply about the quality of the life we are leading as the sun is obviously going to set on our personal existence in the foreseeable future. We joined those with adequate pensions as against those relying only on the pittance of the state OAP. We therefore resolved to make use of our time fulfilling any latent ambitions, projects, journeys or interests while we had the good health to follow them. We also aimed to enjoy such experiences together as it would build a joint memory bank that, apart from just nostalgia, would help to strengthen the bonds for a long time into the future.

You can never swim in the same river twice – the water is different the second time round – so we didn't necessarily engage in anything radically different from what we had already been introduced to, but the experience and the enjoyment were new. Despite having so many activities in common, we were careful to give each other space as autonomous individuals. Mentally healthy people require autonomy and independence, together with times of closeness and intimacy. We didn't fear that getting close meant losing control over our respective lives. Pat played the piano, visited friends for coffee while I jotted down these memoirs or watched Formula One on television. We could both cope with all the jobs connected with the kitchen, the house in general, the car and the shopping as we had both previously lived successfully on our own.

Confidence in coping on one's own seems to me to be a prerequisite for a good ongoing relationship, as we learn to take responsibility for our own feelings and never to project them on to others. Blaming the circumstances we find ourselves in, being judgmental and assuming that the world will adapt to us instead of the other way round, leads to self-delusion and unhappiness, as it never solves any of the problems we face. Pat has this admirable quality of facing the most difficult ones. Her brother and only sibling was murdered in the St Vincent Bar, Edinburgh, in 1984, but far worse was the horrendous fatal accident of her only son whilst diving for a company off the Fife coast in 1991. Some people's characters are never tested. Hers was.

It is of interest to me that researchers have confirmed the common sense conclusions that we need support if we are to have the necessary resilience to face anything that life throws at us. This support is not financial. It includes good relationships with our parents, appropriate connections with communities of interest or place. More importantly, it involves an external value system that goes beyond the welfare of ourselves, providing a feeling of purpose and meaning to our lives. Traditionally, religion has supplied the latter to much of mankind but the straight humanitarian and humanist approach avoids the dogmatism that has made so many religions destructive, as well as comforting, to those inheriting them. Thus, the personal must be social in the first instance. When decisions have to be made it becomes a political issue.

Pat and I do have some disagreements! For example, we agree to disagree on the supernatural and the respective roles of science and art. It seems to me that because we cannot explain some phenomena, it doesn't mean that we have got to invent an answer, frustrating though it may be. The history, especially of the last three hundred years, of the vast increase in our knowledge of the universe, is that most myths, miracles and magical explanations of former times have now been explained but, of course, there is a mountain of phenomena yet to be accorded an explanation.

Pat has rekindled in me a love of music and an interest in the arts which I have often deliberately neglected in the pursuit of what I listed as priorities, as described in previous chapters. I remember, as a teenager, making a list at the back of a notebook of the music I heard and whether or not I liked it. I placed up to three ticks against each one, depending on whether it was 'not bad', 'worth listening to again' or a definite 'must'. The latter included Beethoven's Fifth and Ted Willis and I once went to the Garrick Theatre in Southport to hear it with Sir Malcolm Sargent conducting the Liverpool Philharmonic Orchestra. Prior to that, it was 'film music'. From then on I loved the classics, but rarely went to concerts, preferring, instead, the theatre, opera and ballet – until I met Pat.

Symphonies seem to echo my life's experiences, with quiet and melodious passages followed by bursting crescendos and different sections of the orchestra sometimes playing off against each other. Sometimes there are discords, but I like it when these once again give way to harmony and enchanting rhythm. In sum, I have tried to combine the development of my physical skills with intellectual effort and a passionate response to what I deemed to be social and political priorities such as education and the peace movement. It strikes me that most people listen to and read the works of only the leading authorities of particular subjects and thereby tend to denigrate the opinions of others. Whilst I greatly admire and value all sorts of talent, I think that most of us should strive to become good generalists rather than poor specialists and place a higher value on the well-rounded person.

Now, at seventy, I am slowing down, taking life more easily, looking back, which has never been a habit of mine.

However, I still wake early and my grey matter immediately becomes charged with nervous energy as I open my eyes to a new day. What a wonderful life! I decided to leave all campaigning to the younger generation, and then I recall what is happening to the planet and its people and wonder... what next?

Chapter X
The Future

Every once in a while the dialectic of science carries ideas in unexpected directions that connect with wider social movements, revealing the deeper relationships between the two. Current concerns about health, environment, community structure and quality of life in general (as opposed to quantity of consumer goods) all reflect shifts of focus: from the individual to relationships and the collective, the part to the whole, and from control of quantity to participation in quality.

Brian Goodwin
Soundings, Spring 1997

Tobermory   John Newton
                              9 July 95

This century has seen the best, but also the worst of man's achievements, and I have had the remarkable privilege of living through most of it, observing some of it and participating in a little. We are now approaching the millennium and it is time to take stock.

Let us recall the subtitle of this work: 'The Social History of a Left-Wing Activist.' I now think that the words 'left' and 'right' are inadequate to describe the pluralist nature of the conflicting interests in society. At three score years and ten I have retired from organisational responsibilities, but it occurred to me that the evolution of my thoughts, decisions and actions may be of interest to others, especially to those who would like to put me into the psychiatrist's chair!

I therefore jotted down my memories as they emerged of those decades. It is not a question of ferreting out all the errors and omissions for an extended and revised edition, even though this would not be without significance, for what we forget may also be something we would rather not remember. Professional authors rewrite their texts ten times over, embroidering and embellishing them to make them more attractive to the reader. I know that this draft lacks anecdotes and humour. It lacks humility, style and an explanation of what I really mean as I jump from one aspect to another. It lacks... but why go on? It is for others to judge my life, but I hope, instead, that these memoirs may provoke my grandchildren, friends, political acquaintances and others to think more generally of their implications and, by understanding a little more of the past, understand a little more of how they should face the future.

In these pages I have challenged the notion of inevitable progress, hence the title. We may make personal progress in our acquisition of goods, knowledge and wisdom, and these can be made available to others. For example, there is no going back on our ideas of justice, human rights, animal welfare, the role of women, democratic participation and a scientific rather than a superstitious way of thinking. I have witnessed remarkable changes in the attitude and behaviour of men and women towards each other, derived in the first instance from the increased education and economic independence of women and, secondly, from the collective action of women. These changes have led, in turn, to a 'new man' free to express his inner feelings without being called a 'wimp'. Also, my own thoughts about world affairs have changed but I can point to no one event and say, 'It was then that I changed my mind.'

I hope that these chapters have shown that I have matured through time, experience and reflection and that you should now begin to know what made me tick. But the crucial question is, 'Has the collective wisdom and behaviour of humanity as a whole increased?' I doubt it. Like the holiday crowds that destroy the peace and beauty of places that attracted them in the first place, we are also destroying Planet Earth and jeopardising the well-being of future generations. There is little sign of the political will necessary to alleviate the abject poverty, misery, ill health and ignorance into which the majority of mankind is born.

For me, this century has meant a lot. I see myself as one link in a chain of generations. I have, at last, found out what life is all about. Life is a struggle. It may be for the individual or for the species. It may be Darwinian or humanitarian. I've had my crack of the whip and I am now content that I have lived my life to the full. I would hope that I haven't hurt anyone, but I know I must have done. I've grown up in my relationships, but not soon enough.

Most important for me is that I did what I could at the time – and not just for myself.

I enjoyed making a bold attempt at realising my potential in as many aspects of life as possible. Not being talented in any one aspect, I benefited from a wealth of influences and experiences, from art, music, drama and study, to teaching, travel, gardening and sailing. This is important inasmuch as the previous chapters may have given the impression that my life was spent getting in and out of politics and relationships! Indeed, the ordinariness of my daily routine has been as self-fulfilling as the more colourful days of organising successful events, meeting celebrities or leading the way in geographical fieldwork. What stands out is my relationship with my grandson, Tristan, and our common love of the sea with an enviable and mutual trust and respect for each other's abilities and aspirations.

However, we cannot assume that our closest partners share our values. Pat took the photograph of Tristan and myself, sailing in the Caribbean (see end photo section), then composed this poem as we approached the shelter of the coral reef at Port Morelos, Mexico.

A pleasure yacht on the Caribbean,
The engine roars and splutters,
The fittings rattle,
My head rattles with the din
As I sit crouched below.

The smells of engine and toilet mingle in the nostrils.
The rain and spray lash the deck.
The sun is on a sabbatical
And only the skipper is happy.

He steers the boat
And organises the crew.
This is his bliss time.
The hazards that churn my stomach
Are the stuff of adventure to him.

I can empathise with the Pilgrim Fathers,
Imprisoned in crowded ships
With weeks of landless vistas.
They didn't have engines or toilets
Or the lockers stuffed with food.
What hell on earth it must have been,
And I have tasted only one per cent of it.

*

In my youth I was shy and socially ill at ease, but I was enthusiastic about 'finding out', and this put me in a position of having to change, sometimes superficially overriding my basic character traits. My grasp was always less than my reach however, as I did not always persist long and hard enough in any one direction. Hence, I regard myself as the same person, with the same nagging conscience, as sixty years ago, but with a much more open personality, less impetuous and more contented with my lifestyle.

Throughout my life the personal has been linked to the political, and my attitude reflected the twentieth century hope that the world could be made a better place by the application of rational thought, leading to the increasing harmony and welfare for all its billions of people, half of whom currently live in squalor and misery, while a small minority are obscenely rich, and getting richer on the wealth produced by the former.

The globalisation of the capitalist market has been accompanied by the collapse of the countervailing influence that the Soviet Union may have had, leading to the world domination of the International Monetary Fund and the dollar. Countries can no longer control their own economies. There is an aggressive 'winner takes all' philosophy which is gaining strength. For example, in 1965 the ratio of the wealth of the top twenty per cent to the bottom twenty per cent was thirty to one. Now it is seventy to one. The counter-claim is that there is a trickle-down effect and that even if the wealth of the rich were spread evenly it would be spread so thinly as to be insignificant. This is not so. 'Facts are chiels that winna ding', as the Scots say. If the world's three hundred and fifty-eight billionaires were to distribute their riches amongst the poorest half of the world's population, some two billion and seven hundred million individuals, they would each double their income! It would not be much, but think of what it would mean for their survival, welfare and quality of life.

Unfortunately, that's not going to happen. The world's capitalist economy is expanding and becoming more exploitative. An example of how it works was shown by Dave Phillips of the San Francisco Earth Island Institute, writing about the Californian tuna industry. (*New Internationalist*, February 1997). 'In the old days,' he said, 'California had the largest tuna-canning industry in the world, but today – these are approximate figures – the wages in California are about seventeen dollars an hour. So the industry moved, first to Puerto Rico, where wages are about seven dollars an hour, and then, when they decided that was too much, to American Samoa, where wages are about three dollars fifty an hour. From there it moved to Ecuador, where workers are paid about four dollars an hour, and then on to Thailand, where a great deal of the industry is today, and wages are four dollars a day! And now, amazingly enough, there is some movement to Indonesia, where wages are as low as two dollars a day.' Low, of course, because there is a military dictatorship keeping protest down, with the help of arms exported by Britain, France and the United States.

This is the real reason for 'aid'. The IMF makes it a condition of lending that the recipient countries reduce expenditure on education, health and welfare, but not on arms imports. Yet, only one per cent of the world's expenditure on arms would be sufficient to educate the eighty per cent of the world's children not at school. Another one per cent would enable everyone to have access to clean water that would remove the shame of allowing a child to die every three seconds from preventable diseases.

The present economic system cannot reform itself and there is no indication that a Labour government has the political will to do any better. I was one of many beavering away, thinking that the alternative ideas of socialism would be contagious and, through mass struggle, would eventually lead to them becoming an unstoppable force and so improve the quality of life of all. I was wrong. The disorder, instability, fragmentation and unpredictability of the human condition echoed the physicist's 'chaos theory' rather than Marx's rationale of progress. Marx was, however, correct in concluding that it is not the consciousness of men that determines their being but, on the contrary, their social being that determines their consciousness.

*

To summarise what I now think, it seems to me that we are locked into a global capitalist economy with hierarchical, aggressive and competitive societies, which may or may not be producing more consumer goods, but are certainly increasing the 'feel-bad' factor. The information superhighway is accelerating the take-up of consumerism and irrationalism that, if continued, can only lead to catastrophe – just read the United Nation's report 'Our Common Future', and the many other publications on the rapidly changing face of our planet if you want to know whether or not this is sensationalism!

George Soros, the world's leading financier who makes and loses billions in any one week, says (*New Statesman* 1997) that one day the global financial market will collapse into chaos unless we find 'some international co-operation to match the globalisation of markets.' The danger, it seems to me, is that any future proposal to the UN will be too little and too late without a global movement to campaign for it.

Global warming will result in rising sea levels and more climatic extremes. The hole in the ozone layer will cause more skin cancers and wildlife extinctions. The world is losing seven million hectares of fertile land each year to soil degradation and erosion. Clean water is now more expensive than oil in many countries and will be a source of international conflict as supplies of both dry up. Car production and pollution, already approaching saturation levels, will double in the next two decades. The list grows longer, as does the lip service paid to it, while the movement of economic migrants is already threatening regional stability.

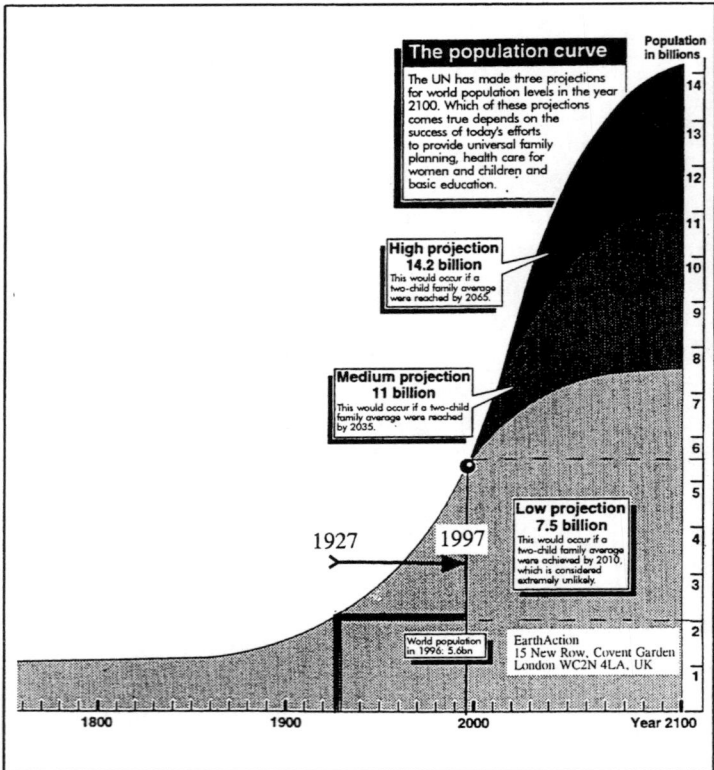

The population curve

The UN has made three projections for world population levels in the year 2100. Which of these projections comes true depends on the success of today's efforts to provide universal family planning, health care for women and children and basic education.

Population in billions

High projection 14.2 billion
This would occur if a two-child family average were reached by 2065.

Medium projection 11 billion
This would occur if a two-child family average were reached by 2035.

Low projection 7.5 billion
This would occur if a two-child family average were achieved by 2010, which is considered extremely unlikely.

1927

1997

World population in 1996: 5.6bn

EarthAction
15 New Row, Covent Garden
London WC2N 4LA, UK

1800   1900   2000   Year 2100

We are now at the end of the twentieth century in which every decade has seen the doubling of previous knowledge, but unfortunately not of wisdom. It has been a century in which world population has multiplied fourfold, urban population sixfold, the consumption of energy and non-renewable resources tenfold – an acceleration of events affecting the world ecosystem and which our planet will be unable to sustain. It took four million years for the world's population to reach two billion in 1927, the year of my birth. Now look at the graph. It has doubled in my own short lifetime!

John Cleese has said that prolonged chaos in society is worse than organised wickedness! We are no longer talking about a new utopia, but about *survival*. What the existing political structures cannot prioritise is that PEOPLE NEED PEOPLE. Instead, we are being seduced into thinking only of acquiring consumer goods to the exclusion of other values. Too many people are encouraged to think that they can join the few winners instead of the many losers. Yet the people I meet know that there is something wrong, but feel impotent to do anything about it.

We are also encouraged to recycle waste paper, cans and bottles and give generously to 'Third World' charities. No one doubts their value, but it is only applying sticking plasters where major surgery is required. At present we are like rabbits caught in the headlights of a car, unable to move. As the *Scotsman* columnist, James Hunter, wrote in January 1997, 'When a plausible replacement for capitalism – in the shape of Marxist-inspired socialism and communism – seemed to be waiting just off-stage, it made good sense, even to capitalism's most fervent proponents, to minimise joblessness, poverty and the like. But now that there is no alternative – no readily believable alternative, at any rate – to capitalism, this most productive, most inventive, but also most voracious and exploitative of economic systems, can safely be let rip in a fashion not seen since the early nineteenth century.'

Therefore, slogans for world revolution will go unheeded, but we can, at least, defend the gains already made, promote a new vision for the younger generation, and appeal, in the first instance, to the enlightened and longer term self-interest of the richer minority. Let them know that if they resist a reform of the system they themselves will be caught up with the problems of disease, instability and violence breaking out as the pot boils over.

Along with many of my generation, I thought that education, not merely schooling, would lead to a greater feeling of responsibility and therefore of political involvement by more and more people. This, in turn, would lead to the development of a mature civic society that would not allow a government to do otherwise than prioritise social need over private greed. Some pointed to Sweden as an example. Others, like myself, thought that social change had to go much further if the resistance offered by the established forces was to be overcome.

My conclusion is that if we are to make the millennium a real turning point in man's turbulent history, we have got to think laterally and imaginatively, but, at the same time, be realistic about the nature of the beast – man!

I think it was Confucius who said that learning without thinking is useless but thinking without learning is dangerous. Can we promote this idea?

It has always seemed to me that theory and practice must go together, and that pragmatism must accompany principle. However, we have an abundance of untenable beliefs that, far from making paths, are blocking the way through to spiritual experiences that are capable of lifting individuals and groups to even greater heights by inhibiting the baser instinctive reactions. A real and worthwhile education must, in my opinion, develop a sense of connection with the rest of the universe in a pleasurable and harmonious way – an ecological approach which should affect the way we think about our place within a giant support system. Only then can we begin to understand how the intricate, complex and beautiful patterns of life work. We may not know why, but we can certainly try and know how, and this has been my fascination with a scientific rather than a superstitious view of the world and its peoples which has intrigued me all my life. I am left with more questions than answers, but a rational view is the only route through to man's survival and his enjoyment of it.

Of course, the conservative view can also be rationalised. 'Human nature won't change. It's a question of the survival of the fittest and the devil takes the hindmost.' As Thatcher succinctly put it, 'You can't buck the market' and 'There's no such thing as society'. All values are therefore based on competition and individualism. 'The less fortunate should get off their backsides and elbow their way in if they can. Their problem is not ours and is not on our agenda for discussion, let alone action.'

This kind of reasoning is very convenient for those who assume that their wealth, power and privileges have been ordained by God. Why, then, should they care about the world's poor and oppressed unless it hits their pocket? One reason is that it is in their long-term interest but they have not yet been forced to think beyond this year's balance sheet.

I have already expressed my views on 'irrational man', but I think it is important enough to repeat my main thesis as summarised at the meeting of the Scottish Progressive Philosophy Group in 1996. It is this:

> If animals don't do the right thing they don't survive, so they tune in very accurately and sensitively to the real world around them. Humans are very much more sophisticated and have the capacity to delude themselves as they

struggle to match their emotional and intellectual responses.

Briefly, the lower parts of the brain are programmed from birth so that we can operate on automatic for much of the time. However, the higher parts involve a learning process, becoming actively engaged in making billions of interconnections in the construction of a very complex model of the world from the images it has received from a highly selected array of messages identified by the sense receptors. At about one hundred thousand years ago, there was a remarkable evolutionary jump with the development of symbolic language as opposed to the concrete associations of animal communication. The new abstract model of the world now inside our heads is the key to self-knowledge, knowing who we are, what we are and the how and why of our behavioural patterns.

This model is then used for comparison when there is further input, leading to action or its internalisation that we call thinking and imagining, but this often comes into conflict with our baser instincts of fear, lust, jealousy, envy, passion, greed, aggression and so on. How often does our intellect accept something that our heart doesn't, and vice versa? How often do people confuse reality with the symbols which only represent parts of reality? How often do religious leaders use metaphors to mystify rather than clarify the moral issues of the day? How often do people confuse

209

religion as a belief in the supernatural with the humanistic needs of ritual, morality, dignity and entertainment?

The problem, as I see it, is how is it possible to increase the proportion of our lives propelled by rational, long-term and global considerations, rather than the irrational, short-term and individual ones? One of the biggest hurdles to its solution is the Platonist-dualist approach that has bedevilled thinking throughout history, that of separating mind from matter, of the natural as against the supernatural; that is, treated as if they were separate entities, and not only separate, but with the assumption that there is an authority or deity with a mind of its own outside ourselves. This figment of our fertile imagination is conveniently reinforced by élites and their reactionary ideologies. On the other hand, the Aristotelian pragmatic view that mind cannot work except within, and as a function of, a living brain, leads to a more democratic, scientific and healthy society.

I know it is an oversimplification to say it, but it seems to me that religion, superstition, legend, cults and mystical philosophies have been instrumental in retarding human progress, but have been part of the human condition because they answer a human need. However, a belief in the supernatural thrives on ignorance and a lack of understanding about what motivates people, and the divisiveness of religions is used by the power-brokers of society in their attempt to perpetuate the *status quo* and its privileged élite. It can be argued that even the most intelligent can be drawn into a belief of the supernatural. Why? I think it is because we are the only species gifted with the knowledge of our eventual demise – and we don't like it!

We therefore hope and wishfully think that there must be more to it than that, and invent a life after death rather than admit what we now know of all living things – they decompose and are recycled with only memories left in others. I say this in a dialectical sense and not in a reductionist or mechanical mode. We are ignorant of what makes self-consciousness and many other aspects, but study, rather than magical conclusions, is the only way to resolve the problems and discover the truth of the matter. In marked contrast to the mumbo-jumbo uttered at many religious funerals, the following quote by Boris Pasternak is often given at humanist ones and points the way to a much greater understanding of what we are: 'However far back you go in your memory, it is always in some external active manifestation of yourself that you come across your identity – in the work of your hands, in your family, in other people... this is what you are. This is what your consciousness has breathed and lived on and enjoyed throughout your life... your immortality, your life in others. And what now? What does it matter to you if, later on, it is called your memory? This will be you – the real you – that enters the future and becomes part of it.'

Humans are tremendously creative and imaginative, producing, not only religious dogma, but also great works of art, music, drama, literature, poetry and, lest we forget, some elegant and beautiful hypotheses in science. Let us capitalise on this. We are rational inasmuch as we can reason, but at the same time we are all driven by instinctive desires and wishes, programmed to survive as an individual and as a species. Many are unaware of these powerful drives, and, as Freud and others have shown, we bury the real reasons for our actions and substitute others. The responses may be plausible to the individual, but they are also flawed and objectively irrational, producing problems rather than solving them.

I then presented to the group, examples of the political implications of this view of mankind and the dangers inherent in the apparent need for 'authority' – a god, a good czar, a leader, a father figure, and media-made icons. It is therefore essential that checks and balances be built into any system.

I ended by saying: 'The question is – to what extent is our future going to be decided by reasoned dialogue, consensus and agreement or by emotive and instinctive reactions with arguments derived from private and exclusive belief systems? I suggest that *we have to cope with an interplay of both.*'

Some years ago, when Adlai Stevenson was a presidential candidate in America, someone in the audience declared, 'Every thinking man and woman in the United States is behind you', to which Adlai replied, 'But I don't want those. I want a majority', and, of course, he didn't get it. The media saw to that! Democracy is a delicate plant and its price is eternal vigilance.

In particular, I am NOT saying that until everybody agrees with me nothing can be done – just the opposite! We have got to recognise people for what they are and society for what it is. I have always believed that what we have in common is greater than what divides us, so let a hundred different flowers bloom. We are all enriched by the pluralist nature of our communities, but let us not bow to those interested in destroying them. It is for this reason that I have found no difficulty in helping to develop campaigns and projects with men and women of goodwill from all walks of life, especially those of a religious persuasion. Many different people have inspired my life, but so too have I been inspired by the story of evolution, the beauty of the landscape, the wonders of the night sky and the challenge of the sea.

So perhaps we might despair unnecessarily as we approach the millennium and I am reminded of Gramsci's edict that the pessimism of the intellect can be overcome by the optimism of the will. The younger generation always had that optimism. The will to change things is as strong today as ever it was.

Can this lead us to a better tomorrow? I hope so.